TWAYNE'S WORLD AUTHORS SERIES
A Survey of the World's Literature

FRANCE

Maxwell A. Smith, Guerry Professor of French, Emeritus
The University of Chattanooga
Former Visiting Professor in Modern Languages
The Florida State University

EDITOR

Charles Fournier

TWAS 578

CHARLES FOURIER

By M.C. Spencer

University of Queensland

TWAYNE PUBLISHERS

A DIVISION OF G. K. HALL & CO., BOSTON

Published in 1981 by Twayne Publishers,
A Division of G. K. Hall & Co.
All Rights Reserved

Printed on permanent/durable acid-free paper and bound
in the United States of America

First Printing

Library of Congress Cataloging in Publication Data

Spencer, Michael Clifford.
Charles Fourier.

(Twayne's world authors series ; TWAS 578 :
France)
Bibliography: p. 175-79
Includes index.
1. Communism—France.
2. Fourier, François Marie Charles, 1772-1837.
HX704.F9S65   335'.2'0924   [B]   79-9100
ISBN 0-8057-6420-8

For Andrew and Christina

Contents

About the Author

Michael C. Spencer is a former Fellow of Sidney Sussex College, Cambridge, and is currently Professor of French and Chairman of the French Department, University of Queensland, Australia. He is the author of a book on Théophile Gautier (1969) and of a volume in the Twayne's World Authors series (*Michel Butor*, 1974). His numerous articles on nineteenth- and twentieth-century French literature have appeared in Australasia, England, Belgium, France, and the United States.

Preface

Although the name of Charles Fourier is now reasonably well known, it is doubtful whether he is read very much. Whether he actually wanted to be read may seem a paradoxical question to pose about a man who devoted a large part of his books to vain attempts at attracting a patron who would finance his "system," basically a blueprint for living in "Harmony," or Fourier's brand of Utopia. When one opens them, however, and begins to grapple with his bizarre pagination, incomprehensible tables of contents, neologisms, and analogical charts, one understands why the question is not an idle one—and also why he never made any money as a traveling salesman. It is doubtful whether anybody ever bought anything from Charles Fourier, least of all his books.

The present study is therefore an attempt to "sell" a still largely unknown body of writing to a public which, because of the times in which we live, should be particularly receptive to Fourier's ideas on education, feminism, and social and sexual relationships, to mention just a few aspects of his elusive message. For Fourier the autodidact had ideas on everything; the major difficulty facing even the most casual reader is whether or when to take them seriously. A large part of our introductory chapter is thus concerned with the complex problem of how to read an author whose works were censored by his disciples, who was declared mad by his detractors, but who today is seen by educationalists, partisans of the sexual revolution, inheritors of the Surrealists, and the Parisian intelligentsia as a precursor of great importance. If some of these seem slightly odd bedfellows, Fourier would have been pleased. As we shall see, everyone has many bedfellows, all the time, in Harmony.

Fourier is usually labeled, along with several of his French contemporaries, a Utopian Socialist. This has not prevented him from being excluded from a recent history of literary Utopias on the grounds that he did not write fiction. The exclusion is a mistake, but it does focus attention on the difficulty of classifying Fourier, and in particular to what extent his writings can be considered as fitting into the Utopian mold, which is a rather depressing one. A large part of our eighth chapter is concerned with situating him in relation to Utopian writers, from Thomas More to the Marquis de Sade, a contemporary of Fourier whose writings offer striking points of similarity and difference. Situating Fourier has in fact turned out to be a major concern of this study, since at first sight he belongs nowhere—perhaps a fitting place for a Utopian writer to be. . . . The reader will therefore find in this book, in addition to discussions of the social aspects of his thought, an attempt at evaluating his literary impact. Charles Fourier, like the Surrealists or Raymond Roussel, transgresses so many of our most basic beliefs about the way language functions that the esteem in which he is held by modern poets and theorists of language is not surprising. There *is* clearly a current fad for Charles Fourier, and it is a mainly Parisian phenomenon. But behind it there is a very real admiration for him on the part of those to whom literary fashion is of no consequence. Our bibliography will attest to this.

This study concerns itself only marginally with Fourierism, or Fourier's thought as propagated, _impoverished, distorted, or concealed by his disciples, or disciples of disciples. To do so, it would have needed twice the space, and a splendid account by Henri Desroche already exists (see bibliography).

We wish to thank the Bibliothèque Nationale, Paris, for permission to reproduce the portrait of Fourier. Fourier's works are no longer in copyright. All translations are our own.

MICHAEL SPENCER

University of Queensland, Australia
November 1978

Chronology

Decides to settle in Paris. Correspondence and accounts clerk for Curtis and Lamb of New York.

1829   *Le Nouveau Monde industriel et sociétaire*, the most accessible of his works.

1832   Foundation of *Le Phalanstère*, first Fourierist journal (until 1834). First attempt at creation of a "Phalange" (Phalanx: Fourier's Utopian Community) at Condé-sur-Vesgre, near Rambouillet. But only some buildings ("Phalanstère": Phalanstery) partly constructed.

1835   *La Fausse Industrie.*

1836   Health begins to fail. Foundation of *La Phalange*, new Fourierist journal (until 1849).

1837   Died October 10. Buried in Montmartre cemetery.

1966   Publication of *Griffe au nez* . . . (homophonous manuscript).

1967   Publication of *Le Nouveau Monde amoureux* (New Amorous World: written c. 1817-1819).

CHAPTER 1

Introduction

I   A Life of Frustration

CHARLES Fourier led an uneventful life marked by solitude, particularly in later years.[1] He never married, appears to have had no lasting amorous liaisons, spent most of his life in cheap lodgings or seedy hotels, gathered—amazingly—quite a few disciples but made no real friends, and seems to have had no distractions. The system he evolved provides unlimited sex for everyone, punctuated—or accompanied—by abundant sessions at table, and is characterized by communal life and constant, meaningful encounters within urban and rural space designed to facilitate communication. It is tempting, and by no means absurd, to see the grotesque plenitude of the one as a compensation for the poverty of the other. Remarking on the facilities—a kind of free massage-parlor service—available to travelers arriving at a Phalanx, one critic has claimed that they are "the fantasy of the traveling salesman who spent restless lonely nights in grubby provincial hotels",[2] while another has commented that Fourier's New Amorous World has all the marks of originating in the brothel.[3] Yet when this has been said, nothing has really been explained, since lonely traveling salesmen, while they indeed may have fantasies, do not (we presume) usually get around to covering several thousand pages with them. Nor (we again presume) do their fantasies take on the imaginative shape, vigor, and coherence of Fourier's.

When he writes about himself, Fourier tends to concentrate on scenes from his childhood or early manhood, in which he plays the role of an individual marked by destiny. The overtones are sometimes heroic, sometimes tragicomic, and the overall effect is to create a kind of exemplary destiny. What is interesting is that the scenes in which the "real" Fourier is presented by what might be called the "writing Fourier" are remarkably similar, in the kind of overtones we may discern, to the many scenes in which invented characters are illustrating—perhaps acting would be a better word—some point the author is making. In other words, not only is Fourier's life to some extent an invention of his biographer, Pellarin, it may also be partly his own invention (he was fond of proclaiming himself an "inventor"). There is nothing new or remarkable in this; nevertheless, Charles Fourier's fantasies are peculiarly hardworking, investing the apparently "fictional" and the "nonfictional" aspects of his works with a status whose similarity disconcerts. As we shall see, it is Fourier's refusal or inability to separate or to create recognizable hierarchies or priorities within his writings that is so bewildering for the reader, who, expecting a treatise on an ideal agricultural community, finds that, while it does exist, it is interspersed with detailed considerations about the sex-life of the planets or references to the author's remarkable childhood. With these reservations in mind, we shall try to sift the real from the invented, or at least indicate where they may overlap.

Charles Fourier was born on April 7, 1772, at Besançon, a pleasant French town near the Swiss border. He was to live through tumultuous times: the last years of the reign of Louis XVI; the 1789 Revolution; the Reign of Terror, in which he almost lost his life; the Directorate; the triumph and decline of Napoleon; the 1830 Revolution. All of these, and the condition of the poor in Lyons were to mark him in one way or another. Fourier was the youngest of the family, having three sisters, one of whom became related by marriage to the gastronomer, Brillat-Savarin. There is evidence that he was unhappy and frustrated as a child: not ill-treated, but lacking a warm, sympathetic family background. He was sent to school at the local Collège de Besançon and did quite well, gaining the occasional prize. His favorite subject was apparently geography; one of his innumerable later schemes was a whole series of new methods of teaching it. In 1781, Fourier's father died, leaving a considerable fortune of which he was to receive two-fifths. Fourier wished to become a military engineer, but he did not have the requisite social standing, so it was decided that he should follow in his father's footsteps. Around 1790 or 1791 he began his apprenticeship in commerce at Rouen and then Lyons. He became periodically itinerant and was never particularly well off, working variously as a commercial traveler, as an unlicensed broker, and in various clerical positions. Thus, having been frustrated in his choice of career, he spent a large part of his life doing something he detested—but talking to people, observing, and gathering a mass of information that would be put to good use in his later, devastating analysis of the commercial world of his day.

In 1793, after a stay in Marseilles, he went to live in Lyons. Whatever did happen to him there in 1793—his biographer, Pellarin, claims that he lost most of his fortune, while a later writer, Simone Debout, suggests that he may have only lost his personal effects[4] —the events created in him a profound dislike of social upheaval and revolutions. The city rebelled against the Convention (the central government) and was besieged in August and September. When it capitulated, Fourier was imprisoned and narrowly escaped being killed in the butchery that followed.[5] Shortly afterwards, in 1794, he was called up for military service. Although he was scarcely of a nature or physique to enjoy this enforced servitude (he was discharged as medically unfit in 1796) something of it may well have rubbed off onto life on a Phalanx, certain aspects of which have a decidedly military ring about them.

Over the next few years he traveled a good deal and began writing. Several short articles and poems of his were published in various Lyons newspapers from 1801 onwards. One of them, which outlined with considerable authority a plan for France's foreign policy, brought him to the attention of the police. Two others, "Harmonie universelle" and the "Lettre au grand juge" both written late in 1803, were a brief outline of Fourier's social system, a kind of indication of what Harmony might be. In 1808, he published his first major work, the *Théorie des quatre mouvements et des destinées générales*, with a false place of publication (Leipzig) and no real indication of the author. Fear of censorship and, according to Fourier later on, a desire to deceive his critics, are among the possible reasons for these subterfuges and the generally rebarbative disposition of the volume. Its effect might be likened to dropping a feather in a pond, and the notice at the end that the next six (unpublished) volumes could be reserved by advance payment to the author

("Charles, à Lyon")[6] was hardly calculated to bring in a rush of subscriptions. The vagueness of the author's address also taxed the perseverance of an early disciple, Just Muiron, who took two years to track him down.

In 1812, Fourier's mother died, leaving him a life annuity of 900 francs, a precious supplement to what little he received from his various jobs. He was thus able to withdraw to the country in the winter of 1815-1816 in order to perfect his theories and to map out his *Great Treatise* (the *Grand Traité* that was never to be written), living first with his nieces at a village called Talissieu and then with a sister at Belley, where Muiron finally caught up with him in 1816. Ironically, Muiron was quite deaf, a fitting disciple for such an elusive man to have. Posterity should be grateful for his infirmity, as their interviews were written down and parts have been preserved. At Muiron's insistence, he moved to Besançon in 1821; in the following year, he published the two- (later four-) volume *Traité de l'association domestique-agricole*, the contents of which bore little relation to the title, which was subsequently changed to the *Théorie de l'unité universelle*. Full of hope, Fourier went to Paris to whip up enthusiasm for his discovery, sending copies and prospectuses to all and sundry, including Robert Owen, whose ideas on social organization bore some similarity to his own. Nobody took any notice at all of him or his books.

In spite of his lack of success, Fourier had acquired by 1825 a small group or school of disciples, among them Muiron, Victor Considerant, and Clarisse Vigoureux, who were to expound his doctrine after his death. The miracle is that he should have found any at all. From 1826 on, and in spite of his lack of success there, Fourier decided to live in Paris. In 1829 he published a slightly more accessible account of his theories entitled *Le Nouveau Monde industriel et sociétaire*. From now on, he began to be obsessed with finding a patron who would finance a trial run for his Phalanx. Unfortunately, he had competitors, since he was by no means the only man of his times to invent systems to save humanity in which the social and the religious, the serious, the comic, and the downright bizarre coexisted in uneasy fashion.[7] Fearing these competitors, he also did what all inventors of strange systems do and published in 1831 a virulent pamphlet entitled *Pièges et charlatanisme des sectes Saint-Simon et Owen, qui promettent l'association et le progrès* (Traps and Charlatanism of the Saint-Simonian and Owenite Sects, Who Promise Association and Progress). In 1832 the first Fourierist journal, *Le Phalanstère*, began publication, some Saint-Simonians were coming over to the Fourierist cause, and the first Phalanx was founded, at Condé-sur-Vesgre, on the edge of the forest of Rambouillet.

Thus, in spite of Fourier himself, one is tempted to say, a Fourierist movement had begun to take shape. His attitude toward the project at Condé-sur-Vesgre is of particular interest in the light of the efforts he had been making to attract a Maecenas. That the whole scheme was ill-conceived is not in doubt; the architect was clearly either incompetent or a lunatic: the most luxurious part of the buildings was the pigsty, except that no provision for an entrance had been made, so that the animals would have had to be lifted in and out by a pulley. Fourier had been cosignatory of a circular letter to newspaper editors seeking free publicity for the project, but his general attitude seems to have been one of distant disapproval. In his last major published work, the tired and bitter *La Fausse Industrie* of 1835-1836, he repudiated the whole enterprise: "It's rumored that I tried out my system at Condé S.V. and THAT IT FAILED. It's yet another calumny spread by gossips. I did nothing at Condé. A domineering architect wouldn't have anything to do with my plan. . . . a mad Anglomaniac, who only wanted what he'd seen in England, or rather his fantasies that changed from one day to the other" (IX, Z5).[8] Fourier was by 1832 old and in ill health, and the project clearly was a disaster. Yet we are left with the uneasy feeling that he *wanted* it to fail quickly, possibly because he wished to keep his reputation intact: the great inventor betrayed by his followers.

From 1833 on, Fourier's health declined. The describer of gastronomic orgies who had spent his life eating bad food in cheap restaurants began to suffer from intestinal troubles. For the last year of his life he was virtually confined to his tiny apartment, declining medical aid and human companionship. On the morning of October 10, 1837, his concierge found him dead, kneeling by his bed, dressed in his frock-coat. He was accorded an orthodox Catholic funeral, which scandalized some of his followers (Fourier was hardly an orthodox Christian) and interred in the Cimetiere de Montmartre. On the neglected tombstone one can just make out the inscription: "Here lie the remains of Charles Fourier. The Series distribute the Harmonies. The Attractions are proportional to the Destinies."[9]

II   *The Price of Apples*

The picture of Fourier left by Pellarin has been somewhat modified over the years. His biographer saw him as a slightly eccentric man, living in his own mental world, very hard-working, basically kindly, and full of concern for others. He loved flowers, cats, and music. Posterity, as is its wont, has treated him more harshly, largely because it has read between the lines he wrote with its Freudian glasses on. He was clearly what the French call a "maniaque" (a crank), splitting matches to make them last longer, preserving pins and bits of string, and so on.[10] He was fussy about what he ate and drank, according to Pellarin, disliking tea because he disliked the English, and bread because he disliked Parisian restaurants. He had an extraordinarily sweet tooth: Harmony, Roland Barthes has observed, "will be candy-coated." [11] A hilarious correspondence preserved in the French National Archives refers to Fourier's requests, without supporting evidence, for payment to him by the war ministry of the sum of 190 francs for clerical services rendered. The requests were made nine and then thirteen years after the alleged nonpayment. . . .[12] The same dossier contains a whole series of letters from various ministries thanking Fourier for his various schemes. One marvels at the polite tone of the replies and their promptness. The projects included a new method of teaching geography, a design for French foreign policy, a revised system of musical notation, improvements in the organization of the army, the establishment of rural banks, and improvements in town planning. This list excludes the considerations on everything that are found in his major works.

Hardly anybody listened to Fourier, and his first disciple was deaf. It is therefore small wonder that most modern critics, having already decided that he was a repressed homosexual with a massive Oedipus complex, should also refer to his paranoia. He complained constantly that he was being unjustly vilified by the press, when most of the time it took no notice of him at all.

Many pages of *La Fausse Industrie* are devoted to this subject, including a plea for the setting up of a kind of Press Tribunal to restrain newspapers from vilifying inventors (VIII, 100-109). He was pathologically scared of plagiarism, constantly writing of his secret and of his destiny (Xa, 1-37): Christopher Columbus, Galileo, and Christ are "precursors" frequently referred to—men who were misunderstood, abused, even martyred, yet who triumphed in posterity. Although he refused the title of Messiah in *La Fausse Industrie*, professing the title *"postcursor prophet"* (IX, 485, Fourier's italics), a fragment published by the Fourierist journal *La Phalange*, in which Fourier annotates a conversation between the poet Lamartine and Lady Esther Stanhope, makes it quite clear that, in his more private moments, he imagined himself to be the Son of God.[13] As the Messiah was not listened to, his contemporaries were punished. In a bizarre piece of self-justification entitled "The Inventor and his Century," Fourier not only claimed that his first book was a "parody" or "masquerade" aimed mainly at protecting himself against plagiarism, but that, as it had not been taken notice of, Civilization was paying at the rate of one million heads per year.[14] In an even more bizarre passage (like the previous one, published posthumously) he prophesied that if his message were not listened to, the planet itself would die (VII, 490).

Although Fourier frequently likened himself to Galileo, Christ, and Columbus, his favorite reference was to Newton, a genius who had been understood. His discovery had naturally been surpassed by Fourier's, in one of a series of incidents that marked an exemplary life. One evening, he relates, he was dining with a friend (Brillat-Savarin, according to those who are not content with Fourier's own embellishments) in a Paris restaurant. The apple served for dessert cost fourteen sous, or, Fourier reflected, 100 times more than apples of the same or better quality at home:

I was so struck by the difference in price in two places with a similar climate that I began to suspect some fundamental disorder in the mechanism of industry [society]. Thus began researches which, four years later, led to the discovery of the theory of series of industrial groups and, subsequently, the laws of universal movement that had been overlooked by Newton. . . . Since then I have reflected that one can list four famous apples, two because of the disasters they caused, those

of Adam and of Paris, and two because of the services they have
rendered to science, Newton's and mine. (Xa,17)

The incidents had, according to the author, begun early in life.
Having learned in school and at catechism never to tell lies, the
seven year old Fourier was taken into shops in order to "mold
me at an early stage into the noble art of lying or *the art of
selling*." When he protested, the shopkeeper concerned told his
parents, who thrashed him, explaining that he would never do
any good in the business world. "Indeed, I developed a secret
aversion to it, and at the age of seven [five, according to
Considerant] I took the oath that Hannibal took against Rome
when he was nine: I swore eternal hatred of commerce."[15] Seven
seems to have been a crucial age for the sensitive Fourier.
Following talks at catechism about adultery, fornication,
sodomy—and the boiling cauldrons that awaited those commit-
ting such crimes—he decided that it would be safer at
confessional to admit to everything as a kind of insurance policy.
The story is related as an illustration of the evils of "Education
in Civilization," Civilization being for Fourier the worst period
that humanity had to endure before moving on to Harmony (Xa,
78-79). As another example of the vices of civilized education, he
cites an event that occurred when he was three. Being left to his
own devices in an orchard for half an hour, he amused himself
by gathering—and in the process destroying—over 200 dozen
apples, peaches, and pears. This would not happen in Harmony,
where children would be occupied almost from birth. Even yesterday, he continues, he saw a child breaking off all the grafts from a
hundred trees and then trying to uproot them (V, 41-42).
Fact—or imagination—in Fourier's writings seems always to be
characterized by excess.

The picture of himself that Fourier draws is quite
self-consistent, if sometimes at odds with logic: a sensitive child,
concerned with truth and principles, making early discoveries
about the society of his time which were then complemented by a
series of revelations in later life. The system he evolved could not
be fully divulged, but nobody would listen to it. Various
problems are raised by the passages quoted or referred to over
the last few pages. That some are manifestations of paranoia is
beyond doubt; the personal incidents are, we believe, sometimes

invented. Many were only published after his death, as if Fourier had censored them himself. If the references to the life are sometimes suspect, how does this affect the status of the text in which they are found, particularly if it is an amalgam of social treatise and cosmic fantasy? In other words, one part of the text may "contaminate," or be contaminated by, others. Is chance alone responsible for the partial or nonpublication of some of the most important works, or do we believe Fourier when he claims that he feared plagiarism; if strategy is involved, what *kind* of strategy is it?

III *Humor, Irony, and Strategy*

Faced with these problems, and the apparent humor of his fantasies, many critics have simply censored Fourier. His disciples began the process, which has been charted in fascinating detail by Henri Desroche.[16] Pellarin's embarrassment is frequently apparent in his biography, which is full of qualifications and reassurances in respect of Fourier's views on sex and marriage. The nineteenth-century editors of his so-called *Complete Works* simply excised certain passages.[17] Later critics have divided into two major camps: on the one side, those concerned with stressing the social aspects of his writings (e. g., Zilberfarb); on the other side, poets, and critics concerned with the question of language (e.g. Barthes, Breton, Butor) who stress his imaginative gifts. This side tends to be far less exclusive than the other, the three writers in question all implicitly or explicitly acknowledging the unity of Fourier's writings, a viewpoint which we share.

On the first reading, Fourier's major works give the opposite impression. *Lack of coherence* seems their main characteristic. The most readable, with a relatively normal pagination and perhaps a slightly less heterogeneous content than the others, is undoubtedly the *Nouveau Monde industriel et sociétaire* of 1829, but Fourier later apologized for its accessibility on the grounds that it was an elementary work (IX, 619). At the other extreme, there is the first volume of the *Théorie de l'unité universelle*, or the two volumes of *La Fausse Industrie*. The first work in particular seems never to get started at all, a familiar occurrence in Fourier's works: it talks about itself, excuses, justifies, corrects, and restates itself so that, paradoxically, the sheer mass of what is said tends to prevent anything being said at all. Fourier justifies the bizarre organization of the contents on didactic and philosophical grounds: ". . . it is the progressive order or contrasted Series . . . the procedure used by God in the distribution of the universe and therefore, because of the unity of the system, one that necessarily embraces human passions and relationships when they are organized according to God's design" (II, 54 [second pagination]).

Our initial bewilderment may frequently be accompanied by amusement, a form of self-defense in the face of things we do not understand. Fourier's work invites such a reaction, partly because of his frequent use of irony and humor when he is attacking the many things he dislikes, all of which are associated with Civilization. On these occasions, we can laugh with him. The degree of subtlety varies a great deal, and heavy-handed irony accompanying a burlesque situation is not uncommon:

A professor of constitutional law was saying to his audience at the beginning of his talk: "Man lives in the midst of free, rational beings like himself." He was indeed speaking the truth for, at that very moment, a body of policemen entered, very RATIONAL people. . . . They distributed a RATION of blows. . . . to the audience. . . . The students replied and the policemen received their *ration* of blows. It was hardly a rational free-for-all, but it was well *rationed*. (VIII, 238, Fourier's capitalization and italics, followed by much more in similar vein)

More effective, although still in the realm of the burlesque, are lists, tables, or series of Rabelaisian proportions and tone: the hierarchy of the thirty-six varieties of bankruptcy (IV, 124), or the more famous hierarchy of cuckoldry:

[In the 5th order, the pivotal, 9 species and 3 types] are the cuckolds *of gentlemanly behavior*: I'll mention one who found the lover in bed with his wife. There are impolite husbands who, in a similar situation, would have taken a stick and beaten the said person soundly. But this cuckold was a good sort of husband, who was *a man of the world* and believed in politeness.

He sat down and proceeded to deliver a speech full of reasoning to the guilty parties. "Why, Sir," he said, "what a fine thing you're doing, you a man of standing who should set an example (the lover was chief of police)." The latter got up in his nightshirt and, going up to the husband, interrupted him by saying: "Excuse me disturbing you, but you're sitting on my pants." The husband got up and said very politely: "You're right, here's your pants." Then he sat down again and went on with his sermon, reciting excellent, very moral precepts. When the lover had got dressed in great haste he bowed low to the preacher and left without waiting for the end of the sermon. (IX, 553, Fourier's italics)

The two examples we have just given are essentially destructive, being, respectively, part of an attack on the concept of rationality and a means of highlighting the social absurdity of cuckoldry. Our difficulties really begin with the innumerable pieces illustrating the delights of Harmony, and characterized more often than not by what Roland Barthes has called a "poetics of rubbish,"[18] or a promotion of the trivial, creating an incongruous or burlesque effect.

A kind of interlude in volume three of the *Théorie de l'unité universelle* entitled "The never-deceitful MELONS, or the prodigies of composite serial Gastronomy" is addressed to gourmets whom Fourier wishes to convert to his theories. In Civilization, he writes, one can never be sure of melons: men usually buy them, and they are inevitably disappointed. In Harmony, this will not occur, since they will be delivered to a central point by the "melonists," carefully classed according to quality, and served to the three classes of humans and then to the animals, again according to their rank (horses first, pigs last). It is God's will that men should be deceived in Civilization, for one of the properties of melon is "ironic harmony." Fourier concludes with one of his favorite pieces of rhetoric, a sneer at the "400,000 volumes proving that Civilization is the aim of God," and threatens to pick the argument up again later, reminding us of an even greater manifestation of God's irony, the rebellious nature of the zebra and the quagga, which will become tame in Harmony (IV, 47-50). A little further on, a hilarious piece on "the Triumph of tough Fowls, problems of bicomposite gastronomy" introduces us to Chrysante, the magnate of the Phalanx of Saint-Cloud, who loves marinated elderly hens. In Civilization he would be laughed at, but in Harmony he finds at least twenty "comaniacs," a kind of club that gives satisfaction not only to its members, but also to those who raise and prepare the birds concerned. This pleasant little tale is complemented by a dissertation on the importance of strange or transitional ("ambiguous") tastes in Harmony. Fourier illustrates this by an elevating story concerning a young man from Champagne who, in 1818, was accused of raping six old ladies, aged from seventy to seventy-five. Fourier highly approved of this: in Harmony the rapist would merely be as relatively unusual as the fancier of tough chicken (IV, 135-40). Finally, again from the same volume, Fourier explains how England's National Debt can be paid off in a year by hen's eggs. To reinforce his point, he sets out, in tabular form, the total amount of economies per thousand million persons if matches and other trivial objects were not wasted (IV, 206-11).

The foregoing examples are "mixed," in that their demonstration of the superiority of life in Harmony is achieved explicitly at the expense of life in Civilization. But many passages, concerned exclusively with life in Harmony are similar in their burlesque, incongruous, or mock-heroic vein: the famous latrine-cleaning competitions of the Little Hordes, groups of filth-loving boys and girls (V, 138-66, and VI, 207-14); the lengthy account of the "Arrival of a horde of roving cavalry at the "tourbillon" ["whirl" or "vortex"] of Cnidus, Capture of an outpost and redemption of the captives," including the lengthy dialogue—a kind of sketch[19]—between Fakma ("the saintly heroine") and her suitors; or the world war of meat pies, involving sixty armies each of 10,000 men and women, who have assembled on the Euphrates near Babylon to try out new recipes:

On the day of triumph, the victors are honored by a salvo. For example, Apicius is the pivotal victor; his meat pies are served as first course; immediately the 600,000 athletes arm themselves with 300,000 bottles of sparkling wine whose corks, loosened and held down by the thumb, are ready to pop. The commanders face the command post of Babylon, and the moment its telegraph gives the order to fire, the 300,000 corks are released simultaneously. Their fracas, accompanied by the shout "Long Live Apicius" echoes way off in the caves of the Euphrates Mountains.

At the same moment Apicius receives from the chief of the Sanhedrin the gold medal bearing the inscription: "To Apicius, victor Y in meat pies at the battle of Babylon—Presented by the sixty empires, etc." (V, 358).

A more complete version is given in the posthumously published *Nouveau Monde amoureux* (VII, 339-78). Significantly, it is far less encumbered with justificatory material than the passage just quoted, which—like all the other examples we have given—draws attention to its own strangeness, and then justifies it in tedious fashion (V, 362-68).

The difficulties mentioned a few pages back are partly connected with the justificatory framework, above all with the apparent status of the passages in question. The initial problem is one of heterogeneity: Fourier has a case to prove, and he attempts to do so by illustrating, in an amusing fashion, his theoretical framework. The piece concerning cuckoldry is essentially an anecdote, and its immediate context is a pedantic justification of what Fourier sees as the only effective means of stigmatizing vice. Molière had failed, he writes, since his plays simply invited young men to even greater efforts at seduction of married women (IX, 549). For comedies are a "simple" method of attack, using only one principle, whereas the only worthwhile method is "compound": "To stigmatize a vice, one must present tableaux which render it ridiculous *in its every vanity* and odious *as a whole*. Such is the effect of analyses distributed by series or scales of ramifications in gender, species, and varieties of ascending or descending order" (IX, 550, Fourier's italics).

This coexistence of pedantic theorizing and comic anecdotes leaves one perplexed. If the intention is to convince the reader that the serial method alone is efficacious, then arguably the best way would be to discard most of the theorizing and leave the illustrations. It might be claimed that Fourier is aware of his own ponderousness and anxious to redress the balance by allowing his anecdotal talent to take over. But here the contaminatory effect already noted may operate in such a way as to destroy the theorizing: if the tone of the illustrations is ironic, burlesque, or mock-heroic, it may well devalue the surrounding theoretical discourse. Or perhaps the tedium of the argumentation is self-parody—or parody of philosophical proofs. . . . In the same way, the faithful melons could be a playful reminder of Bernardin de Saint-Pierre's illustration of the "harmonies" of nature and man by the fact that the shape of melons renders them suitable for eating by a family.[20]

The same kind of problem is posed by the pieces concerned

solely with life in Harmony, particularly those from the *Nouveau Monde amoureux*, of which the only censor is Fourier himself, who chose not to publish it. If they are regarded as private fantasies, then self-parody is presumably not involved. If it is, then its existence points to a remarkable ability on Fourier's part to stand back from his own creation. More bewildering still is his refutation of those who laughed at him because he prophesied that the seas would turn into lemonade, since the refutation is stranger than the initial claim (III, 440-43). This occurs elsewhere in his works,[21] establishing a curious kind of local coherence: islands of fantasy in the ocean of social discourse surrounding them. On top of all this, we have episodes from the "reality" of Fourier's life coexisting with not infrequent, sometimes detailed references to historical reality—within the context of an *invented* past and present history of the world.[22] Putting this another way, the totally arbitrary (the cosmology, for instance) and the largely nonarbitrary (the critique of Civilization), coexist and support one another. We also have a mass of "explanatory" tables that are so obscure that they have to be glossed at length, dialogues and playlets, instructions to the reader and, on one occasion, an invented discussion of Fourier's ideas, based on an actual one, but presented in such a way that it is almost impossible to decide which is which.[23] *Uncertainty* is the keynote of Fourier's writings.

It is tempting to explain the strangeness of this by recourse to the notion of strategy. There are two basic and contradictory patterns in Fourier's prose. The first is the pattern of *deferral*. Excuses such as "I regret that lack of space . . ." (II,77 [first pagination]), or claims that he is only awakening curiosity (ibid., p. 72), abound in his writings. Conversely, within the marvelous *tableaux* Fourier draws, gratification is almost instantaneous. One recurrent scene is the *arrival*, apparently without prior travel (none is ever described) of amorous or culinary armies; tents have *already* been set up and preparations made, so that the fun can start.[24] In short, glorious glimpses of life in Harmony are given and then withdrawn from our incredulous gaze, with the promise of more, and better, later. Is then the basic strategy one of appetite-whetting, a kind of titillation by a process of bewilderment, so that ultimately we (i.e., one of us who is sufficiently rich) eschew the written process in favor of a practical trial of Fourier's theories? For literally hundreds of pages, particularly in *La Fausse Industrie*, are devoted to promises of immediate social and financial gratification in Harmony to artists, scientists, the clergy, even Jews—whom Fourier detested—and above all to the benefactor who would finance a Phalanx.[25]

But to posit one dominant strategy would seem simultaneously to oversimplify and overcomplicate Fourier, whose texts would become charades built on charades, pseudoparody reinforcing pseudoparody, with every nuance being finely calculated. Appetite-whetting has undoubtedly a major role to play, and there is some consensus among critics on this point.[26] The elaborate retrospective justifications for certain passages are probably the counterpart of the self-censorship Fourier frequently exercised. In other words, on rereading what he had occasionally "let through" he felt obliged to disavow it by pretending that it was a charade. Our own view is that two other factors are also involved: his incapacity to organize properly what he wanted to say and, on occasion, sheer bad luck. These may well account for the five different paginations of volume one of *La Fausse Industrie* and the virtual impossibility of counting them in volume two (cf. the pathetic note in VIII, 430/cx-432/cz).

In short, there is, we believe, no overall strategy that can be discerned in Fourier's writings. In theory, the serial principle should be invoked, since it ought to account for their organization. The disposition of Fourier's *textual* space would thus correspond, for instance, to the disposition of Harmonian space, or to the topography of the Phalanx.[27] But in practice, Fourier's works are a mixture of self-censorship, self-justification, didacticism, appetite-whetting, and occasional sheer muddle. Fourier was, we have suggested, a very bad salesman. Sometimes heavy irony and humor can be detected with some certainty; usually the uncertainty of the text prevents this—or a decision whether parts should be taken literally or metaphorically. Self-parody may quite often be suspected, yet it seems absent from some of the grand cosmic passages (e.g., IV, 241-68). At times the text obscures itself by repetition, with the detail of what is being (re)stated preventing other things from being stated; at other times it may devalue itself by the juxtaposition of heterogeneous levels of writing. Faced with these written manifestations of paranoia, we can do little more than "recuperate" as the French say, our recuperation—the means by which "the strange, the formal, the fictional" is "brought within our ken"[28] —taking the form of description rather than explanation.

IV   *Verisimilitude and Recuperation*

There are many ways of recuperating Fourier. One is to dismiss most of what he wrote as nonsense, while retaining certain parts that constitute the "true" Fourier. The trouble with this is that ideas of what constitutes the "true" Fourier are diametrically opposed, with the standard arguments running as follows: "Why did such a profound social thinker bother with the sex life of the planets?" or "Why did such a prodigiously imaginative writer waste his time on social theorizing?" One of the most intelligent attempts at recuperation, which takes as its basis the extraordinary heterogeneity of Fourier's writings, is found in Roland Barthes's *Sade, Fourier, Loyola.* Having described many of the phenomena listed in the preceding pages, Barthes claims that Fourier's books are "without subject": Fourier is a "logothete," an inventor of language, who founds a language in order to say nothing.[29] If only the answer were as simple, for all its brilliance! For Fourier clearly says a great deal. But it is the manner of saying that tends to blur the message, and the detail of what is said that prevents other things from being said.

Our own attempt at recuperation takes as its basis the recuperative process itself. In order to recognize with any certainty the function of irony or humor in a text, we must, as Jonathan Culler puts it, "have formed an impression of narrative *vraisemblance,*" or the level of coherence at which the writer's prose habitually operates. We can decide whether, for instance, the irony is conscious, or whether we can indulge in irony at the expense of the text.[30] But as we have seen, the number and diversity of levels of coherence in Fourier is very large. The difficulty is that, whereas the reader can establish no level of coherence that lasts long enough for it to assume priority and thus act as a kind of semantic measure against which the other levels may be evaluated, in terms of importance or triviality, seriousness or humor, for Fourier himself the problem simply did not exist.

For Fourier was, we believe, usually self-consistent in the midst of his own apparent heterogeneity, and it is precisely his self-consistency that defies all our expectations and thus all the "laws" of *vraisemblance,* or verisimilitude. Fourier's analogies cut across all accepted schemes of classification and hierarchy, setting up a grotesque democracy in which the cosmic and the trivial, the animal, vegetable, and mineral, coexist and explain—"celebrate" would be a better word—one another.[31] Similarly, and *inevitably* (by analogy . . .), all elements of Fourier's writings have for him exactly the same status: the real and the invented, the criticisms of commerce and the descriptions of erotic fantasies, all enter into the same grand design, to explain everything. The most fundamental basis of our reading activity, the process variously called "naturalization," "recuperation," or in French *vraisemblabisation*(!) is thus (apparently) subverted by the genial delirium of Fourier's texts.

That the subversion is only apparent should be clear from our own argument, which is a similar kind of recuperation to statements that Samuel Beckett's plays are descriptions of chaos: in order to account for the apparent lack of coherence in Fourier's writings, we have merely posited a different kind of coherence: one which as it were "brackets" or subsumes heterogeneity. If this seems like abdication, then our powerlessness may well be an indication that we are, as Barthes claims, in the presence of a "logothete" (whose invention does not preclude a message) and that the social efficacy of Fourier's texts should not be measured in terms of the applicability of his system but rather, as Barthes puts it, "by virtue of the violence which allows [them] to *exceed* the laws which a society, an ideology, a philosophy grant themselves in order to achieve self-harmony in a fine moment of historical intelligibility. This excess has a name: writing."[32]

CHAPTER 2

Basic Principles

I *The Problem of Access*

CHARLES Fourier theorized at great length about everything, not always, we have suggested, without tedium, confusion, or elements of self-parody. For these reasons—and the fact that, partly in spite of them, partly because of them, the system is so complex and so complete—any attempt at summarizing his thought or his works runs into serious problems of ordering: Fourier, the enemy of hierarchies and composer of books organized according to his concept of series, is difficult to resume in the way in which the monograph-writer would wish. Like all previous critics, we have therefore been obliged to treat various aspects of Fourier's thought as it is found throughout his works. Even this proves difficult, for when it is attempted, one is rapidly led away from the supposed focal point. The "beginner" is best catered for by *Le Nouveau Monde industriel et sociétaire*. All but the specialist would be advised to avoid *La Fausse Industrie*, whose dreary paranoia is only occasionally enlivened by Fourier's imagination; those who enjoy erotic and cosmic fantasy should naturally read the uncensored *Nouveau Monde amoureux*. Significantly, the best introduction to Fourier in English, by Jonathan Beecher and Richard Bienvenu (see bibliography), which presents selected texts from Fourier's writings, gives only one extract from *La Fausse Industrie* and eighteen from the *Nouveau Monde industriel*. The *Théorie de l'unité universelle* is basically an abridgement of the unfinished *Great Treatise*, a plan of which nevertheless exists.[1] Its disposition makes it an extraordinary token of Fourier's analogical mania and his desire to account for everything.

II *Man, God, and Mathematics*

Always with an ear to history, Fourier begins his first major
work, the *Théorie des quatre mouvements*, with a series of
statements that remind us irresistibly of Descartes. In case we
miss the allusion, he pointedly explains that he has gone far
beyond his illustrious predecessor. It was obvious from the
catastrophe of 1793 (The Terror), he writes, that the
philosophers had found no remedy for the misfortunes of
society. Feeling that he could do better, provided he avoided the
well-trodden paths of the "uncertain sciences," Fourier adopted
as principle in his researches "ABSOLUTE DOUBT AND
ABSOLUTE DIVERGENCE." Whereas Descartes had foolishly
doubted his own existence, Fourier has no time for such
metaphysical nonsense: he is after "useful truths." He thus began, he says, by doubting the excellence and permanence of
Civilization: could there not be an echelon (series) of periods of
history, where Civilization might take its place, not as the apogee
of social achievement, but as a disastrous moment to be followed
by better ones?

The "useful truths" are framed by Fourier's own inimitable
metaphysics. For if Civilization is the locus of his attack, the
roles of Man and God need also to be defined. The standing of
Man within the social order as we know it is, for Fourier,
roughly equivalent to that indicated by Rousseau: Man is
naturally good (VIII, 373) and it is "the order of civilization
which perverts his inclination toward virtue" (Xb, 103). We shall
discuss later in this chapter the unique conclusions Fourier draws
from this simple premiss.

If, in his basic view of Man, Fourier shows himself as a child
of the Enlightenment,[2] he differs from some of its other children
where God is concerned. The Deity is firmly retained in his
system, presumably for strategic reasons: as a handy reference-
point, particularly if Fourier is, after all, the Messiah. But there
is no genuine religious feeling in his work, no providentialism of
the kind that pervades the writings of Bernardin de Saint-Pierre
or even Restif de la Bretonne.[3] Fourier's universe is of a quite
different kind, with God being seen simultaneously as a kind of
abstract principle, like mathematics and music, and also as a
person who is unable to act without Man's cooperation: a very

strange mixture. For the fundamental reference is to social humanity; for this reason alone, Fourier's universe is not theocentric.[4]

God is thus a Prime Mover and also potentially powerless. Nature is formed of "three eternal, increate, and indestructible principles: 1. *God or the Divine Spirit*, the active element and sovereign Mover; 2. *Matter*, the passive and moved element; 3. *Justice or Mathematics*, the regulating principle of Movement" (I, 30, n.1). The five main attributes of God are: "1. The integral direction of movement. 2. Economy of means. 3. Distributive justice. 4. Universality of providence. 5. Unity of system" (VI, 352). Fourier glosses the first as being an indication that all societies are the work of God and not men; the second, that, being the "Supreme Economist" (ibid., p. 269), He must work with large groups and *not the family* (Fourier's italics); the third, that He would wish all men to have a "decent minimum," instead of living in abject poverty as they do in Civilization. The fourth is really a variant of the third, and the last, a token of the universality of Attraction, through the study of which we may find the divine social code (ibid., pp. 352-55). For it is God who has created Attraction, or the direct impulses of Man (II, xli), and if he allowed chance to affect Man's discoveries, he would be destroying the unity of his own system (Xa, 18): Fourier, who attributes to chance his own illumination about the order of society, claims nevertheless that only a *method* can overcome "the tyranny of chance" (ibid., p. 14). In its place, he asserts Man's—and God's—freewill: Man's freedom implies God's, and vice versa. If Man refuses the notion of "passional [*sic*] balance," by which Fourier means his own theories, then both will be deprived of freedom. The main error of philosophy has been to limit the problem of freewill to mankind, and to Man's reason alone. This is little short of blasphemy (II, v-lxviii: "On Freewill").

Mathematics is the handmaiden of God, and it is closely allied with music. In a famous but slightly obscure passage in the *Nouveau Monde amoureux*, Fourier writes of the need for two "compasses," one for the "passional" movement and one for the "material" one:

We shall have as the material compass, analogy, among others that of music or spoken harmony, analogous to the fixed mathematical sciences, whose [i.e., music] distribution is mathematical, immutable, and unitary in all worlds and at all times. . . . We shall have for the passional compass, serial distribution, or distribution by groups and series, which is the collective and individual desire of all passions and the method established by God through nature. (VII, 4-5)

And serial distribution, as Fourier makes clear on many occasions, is always based on certain mathematical rules (e.g., VI, 314-15). In other words, the unity and totality of the universe are manifested through and guaranteed by mathematics, itself analogous with music in its operations.[5] One of the more interesting byways of Fourier's thought is his fascination with certain numbers, or numerology, which he shared with the Illuminists. Seven and twelve, whose importance in music is paramount, clearly have his preference, with thirty-two also a favorite, and on several occasions he expressed his dissatisfaction with the decimal counting system, preferring to work in units of twelve. The reasons given for these preferences are bizarre in the extreme;[6] characteristically, on one occasion Fourier accused of eccentricity those who limited themselves in this way (Xa, 341).

III   *The Movements*

By "movements" Fourier meant the different but totally interrelated domains into which the whole of creation could be divided. The number and description of them varies somewhat according to the date of writing. In the *Théorie des quatre mouvements* (1808), Fourier lists four: the social; the animal; the organic; the material; while an annotation adds a fifth: the "aromal" (I, 29-30, and 30 n.1). Later versions rank and rename them, with the social or "passional" movement becoming the "pivotal" or "focal" one, followed by four "cardinal" movements: the instinctual (replacing the animal), the organic, the aromal, and the material (II, 32, and XII, 160). The last is the only one we know anything about, writes Fourier in 1808, implying that we are about to learn a great deal about the others. He goes on to explain the most important, or social movement, as "the laws according to which God has determined the order and succession of the diverse social mechanisms on all the inhabited globes": a kind of forewarning of the bizarre chart setting out the past and future history of the world that follows (I, opposite p. 32). The description is somewhat modified later, becoming "the destinies, the scale, and the mechanism of human societies" (XII, 160), which is far more comprehensive, implying as it does the detail of the various mechanisms themselves, and not just the order of their succession. The mechanisms of two societies, Civilization and Harmony, will be the object of very close scrutiny over many thousands of manuscript pages.

With the exception of the aromal, the remaining movements are of less importance to Fourier, and their description varies little in the three versions we have mentioned. The "animal" concerns the distribution of passions and instincts to "all created beings" in 1808 but to animals only in a later version (XII, 160); what happens in practice is that, as far as humans are concerned, it is subsumed by the social movement. The description of the organic movement remains constant: the laws according to which God distributes color, form, property, etc. to all substances. The material movement deals in all versions with the laws governing physical movement, and in particular, gravitation. The aromal movement, which appears in the *Théorie des quatre mouvements* (1822) is far more important than its title might imply, for a study of it will be rewarded by revelations about the sex-life of the stars. This is even more interesting than the sex-life of humans in Harmony, which is saying a great deal.[7]

The importance of the movements lies for us ultimately less in the detail or the variants than as an example of Fourier's mania for *classification*: everything has to be fitted in somewhere, with a place allotted to it. One has the impression that if just one thing, however tiny, is overlooked, the whole system will collapse. Which is precisely the point: not only are Fourier's classifications very different from ours, which is another factor in his strangeness, their aim is not to separate, but to facilitate relationships. Fourier, like his contemporary Balzac, was undoubtedly influenced by the work of the French naturalists, mentioning specifically Linné, Tournefort, and Jussieu. But their weakness, he points out, is not to have discovered the *links* between the various classes they identify (Xa, 63). If the social movement has primacy, it is because Man has a crucial role to play; if, through the exercise of Attraction, he realizes his social potential, he will be able to influence the other movements and hence the destiny of the Universe. Conversely, as we saw in our first chapter, if he does not accept his role, not only he, but the planet on which he lives will be punished (VII, 490).

Thus any event, however trivial, will have repercussions throughout the entire universe: "Everything is linked in the system of movement" (ibid., p. 488). The two complementary operations of classification and analogy are therefore of crucial importance, for they enable the chaos of all created things to be *ordered* and *related*. But because of the apparent diversity of the movements, Fourier needed a kind of guarantee for the sometimes startling relationships and analogies set up as a means of asserting their unity. This he found in two principles. The first is the curiously named "ambiguous," or principle of transition, and as it acts as a justification for the more localized relationships, it will be discussed in the context of the series. The second is "the contact of the extremes" and serves as a kind of cosmic liaison element:

There is no more common consequence of movement than the contact of extremes in the material and the passional domain: this truth, which has become proverbial through the weight of evidence, was a compass, to be consulted in the case of all sorts of enigmas of movement. The properties of one known extreme become presumptive evidence for those of the other [considerations on the importance of the infinitely small follow]. . . . If we did not have . . . a role in the management of the worlds, universal movement would not involve the contact of extremes; man, the last link in the chain of harmony, would not work in full partnership with the first, God; there would be neither unity in the system of movement nor proof of the immortality of the soul, which is only acquired by the plenitude and manifestness of the contact of extremes or transitions. (ibid., pp. 465-67)

IV *Analogy*

It is the practice of analogy that exemplifies this principle, manifesting in the process the unity of the universe as Fourier saw it. As Simone Debout has written, analogy is "a fantastic and radical means of demonstrating Man's practical pressure in the realm of things and natural beings"[8] and thus, we believe, another indication of the anthropocentric nature of Fourier's universe. The major function of the science of analogy is the uncovering of the kinds of liaisons that occur, thereby providing a wonderfully imaginative means of ordering chaos, since it is of course Fourier himself who determines the liaisons he then "uncovers":

The moment we study one branch of the evolutions of the stars, we are led to study all 32, because their operations mesh in various ways, depending in all their details on a universal system. . . . [Their] dominant aromas correspond to the 32 social functions or third degree passions. Herewith the table, associated with a particular modulation, that of the fruits in the temperate zone.

Sidereal Modulation of Temperate Fruits

MAJOR OCTAVE

| *Hyper-major keyboard*: pears, created by | { | SATURN, *Cardinal* [*planet*] *of ambition*; its 7 moons PROTEA, *ambiguous* | } 9. |

| *Hypo-major keyboard*: red fruits, created by | { | EARTH, *Cardinal of friendship*; its 5 moons VENUS, *ambiguous*. | } 7. |

MINOR OCTAVE

| *Hyper-minor keyboard*: apricots and plums, created by | { | HERSCHEL [Uranus], *Cardinal of love*; its 8 moons SAPHO, *ambiguous*. | } 10. |

| *Hypo-minor keyboard*: apples, created by | { | JUPITER, *Cardinal of family*; its 4 moons MARS, *ambiguous*. | } 6. |

✕   PIVOT OF THE BINOCTAVE   32.

Diverse fruits in 4 grades, created by the SUN, or center.

K   MAJOR TRANSITION

Peaches, created by the Vestal star, called Mercury.

(IV, 243)

Analogical study is also a means of expanding knowledge, since one analogy leads to another: "Everything is linked in the system of nature; the analogies link up, and knowledge of one leads to others" (VI, 452). The table just given can thus be supplemented by a more detailed one listing the analogies between the passions, colors, musical notes, metals (and various other things):

TABLE AND ANALOGY OF THE SEVEN PASSIONS OF THE SOUL

6	Do	Friendship	Purple	Addition	Circle	Iron
7	Mi	Love	Azure	Division	Ellipse	Tin
8	Sol	Paternity	Yellow	Subtraction	Parabola	Lead
9	Si	Ambition	Red	Multiplic- ation	Hyperbole	Copper
10	Re	*Cabalist*	Indigo	Progression	Spiral	Silver
11	Fa	*Alternating*	Green	Proportion	Quadra- trix	Platinum
12	La	*Composite*	Orange	Logarithm	Logarith- mic	Gold
*	DO	UNITYISM	White	Power	Cycloid	Mercury (II, 145)

In turn, it can be complemented (and checked) by another table relating the colors and the passions, with the addition of black (egotism), and so on (VI, 459). The ramifications are endless, and are encouraged by Fourier, who imagines the whole human race participating in a game of "hunt the analogy" (ibid., pp. 465-66), with everyone winning a prize, since no object, however trivial, exists "on its own," but participates in an immense network of similarities and differences. Thanks to Fourier, the humble tooth is related to the planets and the alphabet (II,76), and the cabbage depicts a certain kind of love (I, 462). Through the study of these analogies, Man will gradually discover the true face of nature, quite literally, since every animal, vegetable, or mineral will there- by acquire *"a body, a soul, a spirit, a face"* (VI, 465, Fourier's italics). In short, the world is *animistic*.

For Fourier himself, analogy was a means of reading "the magic book of nature; its mysteries were explained one after the other, and I had removed its supposedly impenetrable veil. I moved forward in a new scientific world" (I, 12). "Once the unity of the spiritual and the material world had been established," he writes on the same page, "I suspected that this analogy could extend from general laws to particular laws; that the attractions and properties of animals, vegetables and minerals were perhaps coordinated on the same level as those of man and the stars. . . . Thus a new fixed science was conceived: *the Analogy of the four movements*" (Fourier's italics).

If we have come round in a circle, the movements leading to the analogies and the analogies back to the movements, it is perhaps the best way of indicating the immense tautology of Fourier's system (and the difficulty of explaining it without repetitions): every aspect demonstrates, and is in turn demonstrated by, every other aspect. It is this, and the complete arbitrariness of every principle we have examined so far, that is initially so difficult to accept. Once one has entered the system, however, one can be sure that the justifications, or justifications of justifications, will proliferate, the text turning endlessly upon itself in mirrorlike fashion. As Fourier himself writes, quoting Schelling: " 'The universe is modeled on the human soul, and the analogy of each part of the universe with the totality is such that the same idea is constantly reflected from the whole to each part, and from each part to the whole.' SCHELLING" (V, 14).

Some of the passages we have reproduced, and particularly those implying animism, suggest that there is more than a trace of mysticism in his writings: a universe of correspondences, unraveled by the initiate Fourier. Whether he inherited the notion from the Illuminists, and in particular the doctrines of Swedenborg, is not clear.[9] At all events, the initiate was more willing to impart his secrets than is normally the case, for Fourier not only regarded the study of analogy as an important part of the general educational process but also as a means of keeping one's sexual urges under control: "The introduction to universal analogy will by itself suffice to generate studious rivalry, whose enthusiasm will last for ten years or more, counterbalancing the ardor of love from the ages of 15 to 30" (V, 267). As far as we know, the method has not been tried. . . .

V *The Passions*

The final guarantee of the Unity of the universe is provided by the analogy between the laws of material attraction or gravitation and those of "Passionate Attraction" (I, 12). Passionate attraction is

the impulse, given to us by nature prior to any reflection; it persists, in spite of the opposition of reason, duty, prejudice, etc.

At all times and in all places passionate attraction has tended and will tend toward three goals:

1. Luxury or the pleasure of the five senses.
2. Groups and series of groups, affective ties.
3. The mechanism of the passions, character traits, instincts; and hence universal Unity. (VI, 47)

"Luxury" seems a curious word to use, and on other occasions Fourier forges a neologism, the noun "luxism," to describe the first goal. "Physical and mental wellbeing" might be a reasonable gloss.[10] The statement that "The Attractions are proportional to the Destinies," which is engraved on Fourier's tomb, is an indication of the will of God, the "supreme economist," who distributes attraction in accordance with our allotted place in the order of things. The reindeer is destined to live in cold regions, writes Fourier. God therefore does not make him long for the fields and vegetation of Europe: he prefers snow and moss. "His attraction is thus proportionate to his essential destiny" (II, 312). In the case of humans, the proportion is slightly but crucially different, since our sensual and other rewards are potentially greater than our aspirations. If it were otherwise—and it clearly is in Civilization—then our life would be perpetual torment (ibid.).

Our passions have two main characteristics, befitting the natural goodness of humanity. They cannot be resisted, and only sophists pretend that we can check them by exercising our reason, but "reason . . . is always useless when we have to repress our inclinations. Children are only restrained by fear; young people, by lack of money; the lower orders, by the machinery of corporal punishment; old people, by devious calculations which dampen the fiery passions of youth. But nobody will be constrained by the exercise of reason . . . in direct opposition to his inclinations" (ibid., 279). *They cannot be altered, but society must be altered in order to accommodate them* (XIb, 127). This is perhaps the most radical of all Fourier's beliefs, one he held to tenaciously, accepting all the consequences, and in particular the problem of what to do with the so-called "vicious" passions (cruelty, etc.) and sexual perversions. In fact, as we shall see, the problem is disposed of by refusing to acknowledge it as such: for the author of the *Nouveau Monde amoureux*, neither vicious passions nor sexual perversions existed. It is Civilization that distorts and represses passions, making them vicious; civilized education in particular is to blame for this (Xb, 293-97). But if they are altered or repressed, the results are catastrophic.[11] Man, writes Fourier in one of his more private moments, "must march toward the realm of good by submitting himself blindly to his passions" (Xa, 59).[12]

Fourier's anatomy of passions lists twelve or thirteen, depending on whether "unityism" (the passion for Unity) is counted separately or seen as a combination of all twelve, which is usually the case. Unityism is frequently spoken of in lyrical terms. It is "unlimited philanthropy, universal benevolence, which can only develop when the whole of humanity is rich, free, and just" (I, 79). Not surprisingly, the most extended illustrations of its effects are found within the context of the ramifications of love in Harmony (e.g., VII, 313-15).

The twelve basic passions are divided into three groups: five "sensitive," four "affective," and three "distributive," so arranged as to fit in with the three goals of passionate attraction. The five "sensitive" passions (taste, sight, smell, hearing, touch) tend toward "luxury." Fourier's preference seems to go to taste, smell, and sight: taste and smell, because of the role eating will play in Harmony; sight, possibly because of his highly developed aesthetic sense and passionate concern for the appearance of things. Utopia is very much an urban phenomenon: the Ideal City, and Fourier was particularly interested in architecture and town planning. The first priority is to study and then develop the many kinds of sight, he writes, demonstrating that his taxonomania is more than equal to the task in one of his more poetic (baroque?) tables, which classes the transformations of the grape, from verjuice to alcohol, and the degrees of love, friendship, and the visual sense (IV, 356-57). One of the most interesting developments of sight, the "coaromal," would enable us to observe (and hence put to use) the "aromal shell" surrounding the earth, a kind of reflector in which all the activities on its surface are mirrored (ibid., p. 387, note). "Combined Architecture," which provides enjoyment for the feelings of sight and touch, is another example of the alliance of the useful and the pleasant, all too absent from Civilization, but an essential part of Harmony. The ideal city should be spacious, homogeneous without monotony; one's eyes should be able to move freely over every aspect without being halted continually by brick walls (XII, 683-717).

The four cardinal passions, or "groupism" (the second goal of Passionate Attraction) are subdivided into two major ones: ambition and friendship, and two minor ones: love and "familyism." The solitary Fourier has little to say about friendship, which interests him far less than ambition. Friendship is particularly strong in childhood (i.e., ages one to fifteen, IV, 340) and can be further developed by the exercise of gastronomic rivalry, one of the important elements of education (VI, 262). Ambition, "the most magnificent of the cardinal passions" (V, 436), is also clearly one of the most dangerous in Civilization, where it is the origin of discord, hatred, and scorn (VI, 324). Those who preach moderation are wasting their time, since God has "irrevocably subjected us to ambition"; we must therefore "study the methods which he has adopted to make this passion an instrument of high social harmony" (V, 406).

What follows is an excellent illustration of how Fourier copes with the more vicious elements in Man. The concept of proportion is invoked: the relationship between the extent of our desires—boundless in the case of ambition—and the means society offers us to satisfy them. In Civilization, one is urged to moderate or repress one's passions; in Harmony, there are two conditions to fulfill: on the one hand, the chances of success must be multiplied a hundred-fold; on the other, people must be persuaded that they will always have in superabundance the means of promotion and wellbeing. In a stroke of genius or delirium, Fourier therefore arranges for virtually everyone in Harmony to be publicly rewarded in one way or another. If a person has little chance of becoming the one and only Omniarch of the Globe, there will be 2,985,984 "Unarchs" or barons (III, 376); failing that, as everybody is good at something, the most humble member of a Phalanx may well end up as World Champion Meat Pie Maker.

The two "minor" cardinal passions, "familyism" and love, concerned Fourier a great deal, particularly the latter. The former, like ambition, has very different effects in Civilization and in Harmony. Under the present social system, it is a "subversive" passion, since the family group is "formed by a material or coercive tie [marriage], and not by a free, passional association, dissoluble at will" (I, 78); its main drawback is to form a unit too small and self-centered to fit in with the serial design of things (III, 43). In Harmony, it is precisely the serial arrangement of work groups or sects that enables one of the worst features of family life, the tension between father and children, to be avoided. The harmonian father, dashing from one work sect to another, will come across numerous children who share his interests, whereas his own offspring are statistically unlikely to belong to the same groups as their father. Thanks to the resultant phenomenon of "industrial adoption," whereby an adult male patronizes a child or youth with whom he has developed an "industrial affinity," several aims are achieved (Fourier is very good at killing many birds with one stone). Friendship between the generations is stimulated, productivity is increased, and the natural greed of future inheritors, who in Civilization wish for the death of their parents, is simply diluted: just as everybody becomes king or champion of something in Harmony, likewise everybody inherits, all the time (V, 444-61).

Love clearly has a privileged rank in Harmony. "What are the other passions compared with love," writes Fourier at the beginning of *Le Nouveau Monde amoureux*. "Is there any one that can stand comparison?" (VII, 2). Yet it is consistently ranked as a "minor" mode or passion. The difference between the two modes, according to Fourier, is that in the major one, the influence of the spiritual principle is stronger; in the minor mode, the material or corporeal principle is uppermost (VI, 96). He is clearly in some difficulty here, which he resolves rather weakly by conceding that in love the spiritual principle sometimes dominates, "when we leave a beautiful mistress for one without beauty, whose nobility of mind or qualities have captivated us"; love is therefore the noblest of the minor passions (ibid.). These unconvincing arguments are fortunately forgotten when he comes to examine love in detail.

There is a similar problem of classification where "gastrosophy," or the art of refined gluttony, is concerned. Gastrosophy is given an important place in Fourier's theories from an early date: indeed, on one occasion, it is stated to be the mainspring of Attraction (VI, 382). Yet it is never classified as a passion. There are two possible reasons. One is that it often acts as a substitute for love, in a kind of private analogy: for eating read love-making; Fourier is thus able to indulge himself descriptively while not compromising himself in the eyes of his nineteenth-century readers. Today the private analogy is all too public. Another is that the practice of gastrosophy involves so many passions (love, friendship, taste, smell, ambition) that it could hardly be classed separately. This is not entirely convincing, since Unityism is given a place among the passions, although it is the sum total of the others.

The three distributive passions are all of crucial importance in the functioning of the passionate series. The "composite" or "blind enthusiasm . . . is the transport of the senses and the soul, a state of drunkenness, of moral blindness; the kind of felicity that arises from the union of two pleasures, one of the senses, one of the soul. Its special domain is love" (II, 145-46). The "caba-list" is "the passion for intrigue, particularly strong among courtiers, the ambitious, tradesmen, and elegant society. The cabalistic spirit always mixes calculation with passion . . ." (ibid., p. 145). It is thus opposed to the composite. The alternat-ing or "butterfly" is "the need for periodic change, contrasting situations, changes of scene, piquant incidents, novelties that can create illusions and stimulate both the senses and the soul. This need is felt in moderation every hour and violently every two hours. . . . It is the agent of universal transition" (ibid., p. 146). The unique goal of these passions, Fourier continues, is "to form series of groups, to graduate them, contrast them, make them vie and enmesh with one another" (ibid.).

It is noteworthy that of the four cardinal passions, only one, ambition, would normally be considered undesirable, whereas two of the three distributives are characterized by violence and have connotations of undesirability, that is, by "civilized" criteria. Their invention may of itself be a kind of challenge to the pro-ponents of Civilization, an indication that it is precisely the so-called "baser" and self-seeking elements in mankind that are the most productive. Like the Marquis de Sade, Fourier realized very clearly that goodness is seldom attractive; however, he harnessed the dynamics of evil in a very different way.[13]

VI   *A Paradox and a Question*

We have left various aspects of Fourier's theories until later, although they might with justification be considered fundamentals. The most important is the concept of series, but as it is concerned primarily with the regulation of Man's life in Harmonian society, it will be treated in the context of that happy state. As it stands so far, Fourier's system is characterized by total arbitrariness, complete self-sufficiency, and imagination bordering on delirium. As an explanation of how the universe functions, it is clearly worthless and should only be considered in terms of its poetic merit. Yet here and there, penetrating remarks on "civilized" society, and in particular certain aspects of human behavior, should make us stop and reflect. Not least of the paradoxes of Fourier is that his profound insights into social relationships only take on their full significance when illuminated by a cosmology that is arguably insane. Finally, his obsession with *totality* is an excellent illustration of how French Romanticism pushed the rational pretensions of the Enlightenment to an irrational conclusion. In Fourier, the eighteenth-century concern with the discovery of laws governing human behavior or natural phenomena is transformed—almost imperceptibly, because of the frequently pseudoscientific and pseudophilosophical nature of his language—into their *invention*. Or is it all a gigantic parody of the excesses of "philosophy"? For the reasons outlined in our introductory chapter, we are unable to decide.

CHAPTER 3

The Critique of Civilization

I *"The Course of Social Existence"*

HISTORY, like everything else in Fourier's system, had to be classified and tabulated according to more or less precise and totally arbitrary mathematical criteria. The view of history that emerges is, not unexpectedly, quite unlike anybody else's. In a way, it is linear, outlining thirty-two successive periods or phases, yet, in accordance with Fourier's serial techniques, the "course of social existence," as he calls it, is divided into two halves, separated by a "pivot" or "apogee of happiness," with the order of the first half ("ascending vibration") reversed in the second. A jump from the fifth to the eighth phase is possible, even highly desirable, while several periods can coexist. Of the thirty-two periods, the only ones described in detail are the fifth, Civilization, and the eighth, or the onset of Harmony, while the first four ("Eden," "Savagery," "Patriarchate," and "Barbarism") and the sixth and seventh ("Guaranteeism" and "Sociantism") are referred to more or less briefly. Unlike other Utopian writers, Fourier does not depict a state of eternal earthly happiness, for the reversal of the first half of social existence brings Man back to where he began, following which the globe itself will die, along with him. Even so, the human race is still promised 70,000 years of bliss, preceded and succeeded by two 5,000-year periods of "treachery, injustice, coercion, poverty, revolutions, and bodily weakness" (I, table opposite p. 32). In case the period of bliss is not long enough, Fourier arranges for Man to survive the globe's demise, thanks to the transmigration of souls.[1]

This curious and highly poetic outline of history is complemented by a no less original view of Eden, the Fall, and Original Sin, necessitated by the fact that Fourier also believed in the natural goodness of man. In Eden, Man organized himself instinctively into ("confused") series, or groups facilitating the free development

45

of the passions. Five factors made this possible: the absence of preconceptions; a small population; the lack of tokens of wealth; the
absence of wild animals; the natural beauty of all created things.
The breakdown of society, or Fall, was brought about by overpopulation (Fourier was an almost exact contemporary of
Malthus) and a consequent reduction in the abundant food sup-
plies necessary for the maintenance of a serially organized society.
Worse was to follow, since marriage and a patriarchal system
developed: Man had entered the "limbic" period culminating in
Civilization.[2] Original Sin (which is distinguished from "acciden-
tal sin," e.g., Cain's murder of Abel) is identified with this degeneration, but it is not synonymous with chaos; rather, like many
other things in Fourier, it ramifies in a nicely controlled manner.
Militant feminists will be interested to read that the "germ" of
original sin (overpopulation) is followed by "masculine despo-
tism" or the subservience of woman, before it burgeons into its
sixteen "echelons," of which at least half are the result of "inept
modern philosophy" (IX, 816/T9).

Fourier is careful not to paint too rosy a picture of a past
Golden Age, since his purpose is to depict Civilization as the
worst of the four limbic states, in direct contrast to the oceans of
harmonic lemonade that are to follow. With equal care, he emphasizes the deplorable situation of France within the civilized
period, since Civilization, like all other social stages, has four
successive phases, two ascending, and two declining, organized
around a pivot. France is conveniently situated in "phase three,
declining," where she stagnates, being unable to move into the
fourth phase, which precedes various means of transition to
Guaranteeism (VI, 386-87). The innate optimism of Fourier's
social history, each period apparently leading to a better one in
the "ascending vibration," thus has an inbuilt check in the form
of possible indefinite pauses within each phase. How this is reconciled with the precise five thousand year span of the first seven
periods is unclear.

II *Social Conditions in Fourier's Time*

Fourier, we have seen, is a strange mixture of the arbitrary and
the motivated. The confrontation of his outline of social history
with our knowledge of history is a waste of time: they just do not

"mesh," to use his own terminology. Conversely, what Fourier has to say about the France of his day must inevitably be, and always has been, compared with what social historians tell us.

They are unanimous in their depiction of appalling social and economic conditions, particularly where the urban proletariat is concerned. If one can detect a general economic amelioration over the period 1789-1830, this was not achieved steadily, nor did it affect all classes. The urban and rural poor became, if anything, poorer, with the borderline between poverty and actual starvation being crossed, for tens of thousands, on many occasions. Food shortages were frequent: around five extended ones from 1800 to 1830; inflation and unemployment were extremely common. In 1792, out of a population of approximately 135,000, Lyons had 30,000 people out of work; in 1811, the unemployment rate reached 50 percent there, 75 percent in the north of France, and around 30 percent in Paris. Lyons was probably the city most affected by economic crises and social unrest, of which the 1793 rebellion was the gravest manifestation. Child labor, begging, and stealing were rife there, as elsewhere, while many wives supplemented the meager family income by prostitution. The illegitimacy rate was as high as one in three in certain areas, and many children were simply abandoned: by 1826 their number had reached 100,000.

The reasons for this horrifying state of affairs are numerous. In 1788, a trade treaty opened the French market to English goods, with major repercussions in factories in Lyons and elsewhere. Political instability was particularly severe in the 1780s, and the gulf between the rich and the poor widened with the ruin of the middle classes; emigration was widespread; promissory notes issued by the government between 1790 and 1796 became worthless, which meant that the state was effectively bankrupt. Under the Empire, Napoleon's Continental Blockade (1806), which forbade all trade with England, ruined the shipping industry and caused great instability in internal trade, with industrial bankruptcy becoming a commonplace. Under the Restoration, the contrast between the general picture of improvement and the detail of ruin, poverty, and unemployment, remains unchanged. The tardy Industrial Revolution in France was beginning to have both beneficial and disastrous effects, creating widespread unemployment.

The "mule-jenny" or spinning machine, for instance, replaced the work of up to 200 women by one man and a child.

But what compounded the misery of the working classes in particular was essentially a moral factor, for France's economic chaos proved a goldmine for speculators, hoarders, dishonest brokers, and smugglers, in general the seedy fringes of the very large class separating the producer from the consumer.[3] Charles Fourier was able to argue a vigorous and convincing case against the "middle-man" thanks to his own experience as traveling salesman, broker, and counter clerk, and his consequent knowledge of the more dubious aspects of these occupations.

III   "The Crimes of Philosophy"

Fourier's attack on Civilization concentrates on its "immorality" and has as its main targets, commerce, and the middle-man. But he also felt it necessary to demolish the religious, ethical, and philosophical framework within which the middle-man was bound to flourish: Fourier's concern with the homogeneity of his own system was paralleled by an insistence on the coherence of the enemy, even if it was a coherence formed by a series of inconsistencies. So, with his customary autodidact's self-confidence, he proceeded to dismiss every aspect of Civilization. The attack is seldom sustained, except in *La Fausse Industrie*, and the elements have to be culled from many volumes.

Fourier's critique of Civilization emphasizes its contradictions and the duplicity of those whose interest lies in maintaining the status quo: moralists, priests, economists, politicians, and the middle-men spawned by a commercial society. In Civilization, the individual is at odds both with society and with himself. In a piece entitled "The Vicious Circle of Civilized Work," Fourier demonstrates the *"clash of collective and individual interests. Every person who works is at war with the general body, and ill-disposed towards it because of self-interest"* (VI, 33, his italics). The individual is at war with himself because his passions and instincts are stifled by established morality, religion, and the social order (VIII, 397/bn). Treatises on morality abounded in the early nineteenth century, and Fourier spares no irony at their expense. In 1803, a newspaper lamented that only seventeen had been published in France; if one adds those published in other countries "actively engaged in the moral trade," writes Fourier, the number must be nearer forty. As they are all contradictory, one would have to change one's morality at least forty times a year (ibid., p. 162).[4]

Established religion is naturally in league with the moralists and philosophers. Fourier, the author of a violent but unpublished attack on the Catholic Church,[5] complains elsewhere in more general terms of the lazy priests who "delude us with the so-called charm of religion in the midst of the hardship and austerity of this life, although they love something quite different from the hardships. In short, the prelates, while they are doing themselves proud in their palaces, return to us, in the form of a twofold illusion [i.e., the necessity of present hardship followed by Paradise], the booty they have taken from the masses" (Xa, 210).[6]

As Civilization was only a painful phase to be endured before one passed on to better things, it was natural that Fourier should be impatient with the cult of perfectibility and progress, widespread in the early nineteenth century, and an indication of the powerful influence of the Enlightenment. Writers and artists were divided in their attitude toward progress, marking very clearly the divergent paths of French Romantic thought. On the one hand, those like Hugo believed that Man could build a better society; on the other, there were those like Théophile Gautier, who was as scornful as Fourier of what he considered to be empty slogans. Fourier's position in the context of these two well-known stances is curious, for he is basically on the side of Hugo. His means of building a better society are however totally different from those of the author of "Pleine mer—Plein ciel." For Hugo, material advancement depended on Man's spiritual progression.[7] For Fourier, Man's perfection was as it were "in suspense," waiting to be released by social reorganization. The blueprint for reorganization itself is quite unique: keep Man just as he is, retain many of the basic institutions of society, including private property, introduce a serial organization of work and pleasure, and Harmony will have arrived.[8]

The "philosophers," on the other hand, by whom Fourier meant not only philosophers, but economists, moralists, and all men of learning, prop up the rotten framework of Civilization by their insistence that everything is getting better all the time:

Who are the real ignoramuses? it isn't the Brothers who modestly teach people to read and write; they don't delude themselves that they're ON A SUBLIME COURSE LEADING TO RAPID PROGRESS TOWARDS PERFECTIBILIZING PERFECTIBILITY.

The true leaders of the ballet of obscurantism are those fine minds that want to teach what they don't know, the laws of social movement. . . . If we pass from the framework to the details, we'll find our philosophers as ignorant about the parts as about the whole. . . . That the philosophers should have failed when faced with the great problem of improving the lot of the working classes should not be surprising; their apparent solicitude for the people is a charade in which nobody believes any more than they do themselves. . . . (IX, 753/D7-54/E7, Fourier's capitalization)

To these slogans can be added those of 1789, the year in which philosophy "intervened to correct God's work and repress the passions" (XIa, 339). Philosophy may well flaunt the word *liberty*, "but it forgot that in civilized societies freedom is illusory without the individual wellbeing of the people"; *equality of rights* is another illusion, since "the first right of man is the right to work and to a *decent minimum*"; as for *fraternity*, the word itself is repugnant because of "the memory of the horrors for which the word acted as a mask."[9] The French Revolution solved nothing, but at least the "volcano that erupted in 1789 and which threatens fresh eruptions" can be taken as a divine indication of the vanity of our legislative measures and the necessity to try out "compound attractive industry," or Fourier's system (VIII, 133).

The Foreword to *La Fausse Industrie* is entitled "The Crimes of Philosophy," and two main reproaches are levelled against it here and in other works. First, it is dishonest, seeking to veil the incoherence and duplicity of the established social order by a veneer of obscurantism. To take just one specific example, philosophy has betrayed poor young women by trying to persuade them that they should remain virgins, knowing full well that many have little chance of marriage. If they believe what philosophy says, they lose their chances of sensual pleasure in their youth and the art of luring some idler into marriage. Any philosopher of good faith should tell women this; instead, "they get together to deceive, to lull [women] with their . . . rainbow style" (Xb, 223-24). Second, philosophy wishes to "*repress, suppress, compress*" the twelve mainsprings of the "universal soul" (passions, instincts, sympathies, rivalries, tastes, etc.) because of its false view of progress. Material advancement is simple and illusory, whereas advancement to Harmony can only be achieved by a "compound" progress of the passions and industry (VIII, 57). Philosophy, like all the other "uncertain" or "false" sciences (the list includes every branch of learning, IX, 762/N7-65/Q7), is, to quote a metaphor that gets splendidly out of hand, "a Pandora's box, a vicious circle that leads from one abyss to another" (VIII, 818/V9).

As the term "philosophers" also embraced politicians and economists, they too are not spared Fourier's heavy irony. A long attack on politics and commerce written in 1803 (Xa, 217-316) again emphasizes the moral duplicity of the established system:

[Politics] is the science charged with curing the suffering of the social body. In keeping with its charlatanism, it accepts the task without worrying about how to fulfill it; it lulls us with illusions and deludes itself that it can substitute opulence and peace for the poverty and revolutions from which we suffer. (p. 217)

Highly treacherous, lacking in daring, devoid of genius, grovelling before vice, its plans are invariably dictated by fashion, impulse, chance, and flattery, and never by what reason would decide as being most appropriate to the nature or interest of the nations adopting them. (pp. 310-11)

Perhaps its worst failing is shown up by the widespread nature of poverty. It is no use talking of *freedom* and *equality*: "The people are more reasonable than you think: they will agree to subservience, inequality, slavery, provided you find the means of helping them when social pressures or malpractices deprive them of work, reducing them to famine, shame, and despair" (p. 222). Freedom, writes Fourier in a combined attack on politics and economics, is impossible in Civilization, since it must be founded on "compound" wealth, the art of enriching both the taxpayer and the state. But Civilization is just too poor (Xb, 5). The remedy for this is first to increase production twenty-fold (VIII, 16): one of the many absurdities of Civilization is that it has produced a very large, highly protected class (the capitalists) which consumes without producing (VI, 547). Second, the tax system must be reorganized. It is laughable to expect the people "to pay its taxes with joy," which is a pious phrase used in a recent "universal catechism of morality". In Harmony this will

naturally be possible. Lucas—one of the favorite characters in
Fourier's *tableaux*—will be overjoyed to pay his annual taxes,
since he will simultaneously receive a large bonus which is his
share of the Phalanx's inevitable excess of income over expendi-
ture (VIII, 23).

It should already be clear that Fourier's economic theories and
his attack on civilized economics are not exactly sophisticated.
The most basic question in economics was, he wrote, "the art of
maintaining the population at a level below that of the resources
available for consumption." In Civilization this is impossible,
because of the need to maintain large armies and the feelings of
repugnance that work arouses in the masses (Xa, 158). Why
should one work when—quite apart from the appalling conditions
—the relative weight given to capital, work, and talent encourages
idleness and dishonesty? Another character, the peasant Jeannot,
illustrates Fourier's point. In Civilization, his talent will be ignored, and he has no capital. As he produces everything, he will
gaily steal what he can from his employer who, in turn, will
extract all he can out of him: "such is the balance of passions in
the civilized state, a war of pillage and cunning called perfectibility." In Harmony, his talent will be recognized and he will have
some property, while benefitting, like Lucas, from annual dividends calculated so as properly to account for his talent (VI,
311-12). "Laissez-faire" economics does not concern itself with
such niceties, since it gives total power to merchants, believing
that they cannot but work for the public good. In short, economics has abdicated all responsibility and bound itself to the chariot-
wheel of commerce (XIa, 84).

IV   *Commerce*

Commerce is "a method of exchange in which the vendor has
the right to cheat with impunity and to determine himself, without
independent arbitration, the profit he should receive. The vendor
is thus judge of his own case and the purchaser is deprived of any
guarantee against the vendor's rapacity and dishonesty" (XIa,
16). In Civilization, its particular form is that of free competition,
or chaos, in which the activities of the Jews,[10] the proliferation of
shopkeepers, commercial travelers, brokers and the like simply
mean that profits are low, bankruptcies frequent, and the pro-

ductive workforce is vastly reduced. At a time when all kinds of economies are being effected, with chicory replacing coffee, and—horror of horrors—beetroot taking the place of sugar, nobody has realized that the real economy is "the economy of hands."[11] Conversely, overproduction of both food and manufactured goods is a frequent phenomenon of a capitalist economy. Fourier, with his particular interest in the cloth trade, recounts how, in 1825, America was swamped with three or four years' supply of clothes manufactured in Europe, resulting in sales at a loss and bankruptcies among vendors (VI, 393). Industry has of course an answer to this by deliberately manufacturing shoddy products: "One can only find *progressive* goods, pretty to look at but worthless, such as clothes whose color changes in a few days, or which have to be returned the day after purchase to have buttons and pockets sewn on again. The grocer sells progressive sweets, without sugar in them. The children to whom they're given on New Year's Day won't eat them" (VIII, 328, n. 1, Fourier's italics).

But the worst effect of anarchy in production and distribution is the encouragement of hoarding and speculation, which Fourier analyzes in minute detail and with obviously first-hand knowledge. Hoarding and its "brother," speculation, are the most odious of the "crimes of commerce," since they always hit hardest at those who suffer most from shortages, the poor. Hoarders are like "a band of torturers roaming a battlefield, tearing and enlarging the wounds of the injured" (I, 237). Hoarding of foodstuffs is one of the best-known and worst forms, continues Fourier, whose writings are full of accounts of how millions are made overnight by hoarding and speculation. It is, however, characteristic of the theorist of the "contact of the extremes" that one of the most picturesque examples of hoarding should come from the village market place. Fourier recounts how a speculator bought up a cartload of buckets at a village fair and then sold them to the peasants at an outrageous price, as he had the monopoly of that particular produce: "Thus commerce is, on a small or a large scale, a parasite which, under the pretext of creating circulation, obstructs it, insinuating itself between producer and consumer, holding them up to ransom and devouring them" (VIII, 312).

Three other evils of commerce frequently denounced by Fourier are bankruptcy, money-lending, and slavery. Bankruptcy is a dual evil; on the one hand, the small businessman may be driven to it by the mechanisms of overproduction, hoarding and speculation. On the other, most species of bankruptcy described by Fourier seldom harm anyone, least of all the rich bankrupt, and are surrounded by the moral double-talk so characteristic of Civilization:

The arranged bankruptcy is the one in which the creditors are gathered together in secret, informed mysteriously of the debtor's difficulties, and asked to agree to receiving half their due, in order to avoid the scandal of a lawsuit, more costly than ever. . . . Whereupon the majority of creditors, who have done very well over the years along with the bankrupt party, agree to this modest 50 percent reduction. . . . It's what I call an arranged bankruptcy. It's very economical, very rapid, and very suitable for young speculators who want to recoup themselves by its frequency, for it can be repeated every two or three years. In this respect it's very well in keeping with the spirit of the times, exemplified by young men of thirty who've already had three wealthy bankruptcies, which bodes well for the future. Hence people say when they see such a person: "He's very young to be so famous!" (XIa, 60 n.1)

Bankruptcy is in fact the quickest way of making a fortune, Fourier writes elsewhere: the best method of doubling two million francs is to borrow eight million. It doesn't matter if you lose the sum you started with, since you only repay half the borrowed amount over a period of years, and you end up with twice the original sum (I, 230).[12]

The tone of badinage so frequently adopted by Fourier when describing bankruptcy is replaced by indignation in his analyses of moneylending and slavery, since they are crimes affecting the poor. In the case of usury, one vice is attended by another, since duplicity is involved as well. It is not sufficient for the peasant proprietor to have to borrow at a rate so exorbitant that within three years the moneylender acquires his property. For him to accept the contract, he must be persuaded that the rate of interest is a third of what it really is (VIII, 422/cp). As for slavery, in Civilization it is worse than in Antiquity or in South America. In Sparta, the slaves thrived physically, and if slaves died in the mines of Peru it was because of the unhealthy working conditions. But outdoor work should harm nobody: 'It was left to the spirit of commerce to kill a race by overwork, because it costs less to buy Negroes than to raise their children" (Xa, 245). Efforts at abolition, or philanthropic plans to purchase the freedom of slaves, are ineffectual or hopelessly expensive. The principle of "industrial attraction" alone will succeed, for a fraction of the expense, if only someone can be persuaded to try it, concludes Fourier rather plaintively (VIII, 64).

V   *The Masses*

Slavery is an emotive word, and Fourier does not hesitate to use it to describe the conditions of the working classes in France and England: "The mercantile spirit. . . . tends to cover the torrid zone with black slaves wrenched from their own country, and the temperate zone by white slaves, by industrial prisons, a custom born in England which mercantile greed gradually adapted to all countries" (VI, 534). On more than one occasion, Fourier describes in detail the fate of the urban and rural poor. Long hours,[13] boring, fatiguing tasks in wretched surroundings, with resultant ill health: the familiar story is recounted with indignation. Fourier relates how "the French workers are so poor that in highly industrialized provinces like Picardy, between Amiens, Cambrai and Saint Quentin, the peasants have no bed in their earthen huts. They make up a bed with dried leaves which in winter turn into a compost-heap full of worms, so that when they get up fathers and children pull the worms off their bodies" (VI, 30-31).

Although we have no reason to doubt the sincerity of his indignation, Fourier's critique of working conditions in Civilization needs to be placed in careful perspective. It is far less sustained than accounts by writers such as Michelet[14] —or Fourier's own descriptions of speculators' machinations and the evils of civilized marriage. Nor is it characterized by the verve that is so common in such descriptions: Fourier may have felt indignation at the conditions of the poor, but it was not attended by the same degree of fascination as his descriptions of the operations of middle-men. He was careful never to sentimentalize in the manner of Dickens or Hugo, and it has been rightly pointed out that he had no time for the myth of peasant gentility.[15] He condemns the work ethic, not because he does not believe in work, but because of the conditions degrading it. Fourier detested idleness; in Harmony every-

body works very hard indeed. But the word "work" has lost all
its civilized connotations, becoming indistinguishable from creative, frequently erotic leisure. For this and other reasons, Marx
and Engels, in spite of their admiration for Fourier, had certain
reservations about his theories.[16]

VI   *The Family and Marriage*

Fourier's writings abound in denunciations of the "falsity and
immorality of the family group" (VIII, 188). Pages of tables and
catalogs listing and describing the social evils of marriage vie in
their humor and verve with the hierarchies of bankruptcy. The
editors of Fourier's manuscripts entitled one section "Commerce
and Marriage" (XIa, 249), a highly suitable choice, since marriage
was for him a commercial transaction involving similar kinds of
fraud and exploitation. Bankruptcy and adultery were for him
closely associated, since both enjoyed the same legal and public
protection (ibid.).

Marriage, the "pivot" of the social system, is a major impediment to the proper functioning of society by virtue of its size: no
community formed of basic units of two can ever hope to work. It
is also characterized by an absence of freedom and by disparity of
taste in the partners (VI, 57). A "scale of the misfortunes of
marriage" (IV, 69-77) lists sixteen in all. Among them are: "the
chance of unhappiness" in which marriage is described as a game
of dice in which the stakes are a lifetime's felicity or misery; the
frequent incompatibility of husband and wife; monotony, especially for wives; the dispersal of children when they grow up;
adultery; sterility; false paternity; and widowhood (by which
Fourier generally seems to imply male widowhood and the necessity for widowed fathers to work and to look after their children).
A rather different list of "subversive properties of marriage"
concerns itself in particular with the motives of those engaging
themselves in this false contract. Thus "internal masculine depravation" is the name given to the means by which men gain
public approbation of a financially beneficial marriage contracted
in the most dubious fashion. "Simple feminine depravation" is
the female libertine's answer to the male practice, while "collective
posterior depravation" is the public violation of conjugal laws by
both parties, or double adultery . . . and so on (ibid., 97-121).

Two major victims of the married state in a paternal society are fathers themselves and unmarried females with no financial resources. The civilized father, as Fourier sees him, is in a perpetual state of cuckoldry, the object of his male children's hatred, mainly because of the inheritance laws (IV, 77-85), and overwhelmed by work and family responsibilities (VI, 264-65). One answer to this state of affairs has already been noted: the practice of "industrial adoption."[17] Another is a tax on bachelors and "pseudomarrieds," worked out, in inimitably detailed manner, according to their age and social standing (IV, 88-89). This has its counterpart in the case of unfortunate unmarried women; Fourier proposed a "virgins' insurance fund" for those who had fallen victim to libertine bachelors or speculators (Xb, 17), since it is woman who comes off worst under the present commercial and patriarchal system of family and marriage:

DEGRADATION OF WOMEN IN CIVILIZATION

Can one find the shadow of justice in the fate that has befallen them! Is not a young woman a commodity put up for sale to whoever wishes to negotiate her purchase and sole possession? . . . People try to persuade her that her chains are made of flowers, but can she doubt her degradation, even in countries gorged with philosophy, like England, where men enjoy the right to lead their wife to market with a rope round her neck and to sell her like a beast of burden to whoever is willing to pay his price? . . . In France, her slavery is fundamentally the same. There, as everywhere, girls languish, fall ill, and die because they cannot have a relationship, demanded by nature, but which prejudice forbids them to have, under pain of dishonor, before they have been legally sold. . . . As a general rule: *Social progress and changes of* [social] *period occur in accordance with the progress women make towards freedom, and the social order becomes decadent in accordance with the reduction of women's freedom. . . .* In short, *the extension of women's privileges is the general principle of all social progress.* (I, 130-33, Fourier's italics)

In spite of this, Fourier's picture of civilized woman is no more sentimental than that of the working class, for a detailed account of female treachery within and outside marriage follows. But this does not mean that we should condemn woman: "Judging women by the vicious character they develop in Civilization is like . . . judging beavers by the dullness they manifest in captivity, whereas in a state of freedom and combined labor they become the most intelligent of all the quadrupeds" (ibid., 147). Women, in fact, have shown themselves to be superior to men when they have been given the opportunity to exercise power, witness the seven out of eight who have reigned, with or without a husband:

And you, sex of oppressors, would you not surpass all the shortcomings for which women are blamed, if a servile education had molded you, like them, to think of yourselves as automatons designed to obey prejudice and to cringe before a master imposed on you by chance? Have you not seen your claims to superiority confounded by Catherine [the Great], who trampled on the male sex? (ibid., 148)

But even Catherine did nothing to free women, continues Fourier. If only someone had understood the example of Tahiti, and realized that true progress could only be found in the combination of free love relationships (with the concomitant freedom of women) and work on a large scale. Since nobody has ever tried out the kind of remedy Fourier envisaged, man has remained *"twenty-three centuries too long. . . .* in the darkness and horror of philosophy and civilization" (ibid., 150-51, Fourier's italics).

VII   A Static Analysis?

On many occasions Fourier invokes nature: not the *natura naturata*, for which, as a city-dweller, he had little time,[18] but *natura naturans*, nature in its unity. "Nature is never false in the *collective* impulses it gives the human race," he wrote (III, 201), and as such, it is in direct contrast with Civilization (V, 47). Statements such as these, and his analyses of the contradictions of Civilization enable us to draw up the following table of equivalences:

civilization		morality		repression of passions
vs.	=	vs.	=	vs.
harmony		nature		proliferation of passions

It is on this simple implicit equation that Fourier's innumerable contrasts between Civilization and Harmony depend.

It could be argued that the sheer simplicity of this misses the most crucial point of all: the development of industrialization on a massive scale and, even more important, the organization of the proletariat and the concept of class war. Does not Fourier's concern with commerce blind him to more important social considerations? On the other hand, industrialization came far later to France than to England, and Fourier was writing about the conditions of workers around the turn of the century. This is, however, the source of our worry. *La Fausse Industrie* was not published until 1835-1836, or more than forty years after the events Fourier had lived through in Lyons. Yet his analysis of civilized society does not change or develop in any important respect between 1803, when he first wrote about the conditions of the poor,[19] and just before his death. Although the equation is ours it does reflect, we believe, an important, *static* aspect of a basically Utopian writer, concerned with perfecting a message that changes little over forty years, and unconcerned with signs of potential social change—other than those he invents himself. Having convinced himself that France was stagnating, Fourier invented a system, full of tables and scales, that would enable stagnation to be part of his *own* design for progress. Therein lies yet another aspect of this remarkable man: for there is within his work, we believe, a constant tension between stasis and proliferation, which manifests itself particularly in his concern with analogical and serial organization.[20] This is an observation, not an excuse. At the same time, Fourier's analysis of the human condition is based on moral—and psychological—factors that are arguably permanent. With or without the class war, Man's passions remain the same. A tentative and perhaps not very satisfactory reply to Marxist critics would therefore be that the class war is a secondary consideration alongside the far more important task of changing society by peaceful means so that it can harmonize with our passions. How Fourier envisaged this and to what extent his proposals are convincing, will be discussed in the next two chapters.

CHAPTER 4

Life on a Phalanx

I The Passionate Series

THE Phalanx is the small community in which people will live in Harmony. Its ideal size is 1,620 men, women, and children. This figure is sometimes increased, but more often reduced, particularly in later years, when Fourier became more and more desperate in his attempts to find a benefactor. In a manuscript dated 1820, he outlines three kinds of "Association": "large" (1,200-1,300 members), "medium" (500-600) and "simple" ("thirty or forty poor families"), although later on the same page he writes that around one hundred families will be necessary for man's transition to Harmony (Xa, 4-5). The minimum size of a simple or "reduced" Phalanx is usually given as three hundred, and Fourier proposed on more than one occasion to have a trial run with that number of children, who were more amenable than adults to being formed into the groups and series necessary for the economic and social transformation of the community.[1]

The calculation of size is indeed quite crucial. Smaller phalanxes would work well enough to persuade people to try bigger ones, but were only a transitional measure justified on pragmatic grounds. Conversely, on no occasion did Fourier put the ideal number higher than two thousand. The basis of the ideal number is 810, an arbitrary figure forming part of a series of analogies with the human body, since there are, he claims incorrectly, 810 muscles in the male and female couple (VII, 459: there are actually 450 pairs in each body). But the main "justification" of the figure is the size of the *social* body, of which the twelve passions are part. No one person has them all developed to the same degree: "The twelve radical passions are subdivided into a multitude of nuances which are more or less dominant according to the individual. Accordingly there are an infinite number of characters, but which can be brought down to 810 principal ones" (I,

83-84). In other words, what Fourier calls elsewhere the "integral man" (XIb, 320) or, in less sexist terms befitting the context of the *New Amorous World*, the "integral soul" (VII, 458), is formed of a large number of parts, which, while contributing towards the whole, are infinitely precious in themselves. The serial method is the means whereby they are combined so as to permit each person to develop his "passional" potential while simultaneously fostering the "industrial" and passional wellbeing of the community. Not only are characters taken into consideration by Fourier's taxonomy, but also age, sex and social standing; the result is a detailed blueprint for Harmonian life, from the cradle to old age (death on the Phalanx is never discussed).

Thus the "Large Scale Phalanx" will contain, for instance, 180 children below the age of three, subdivided into three age groups — nurselings, babies, and "imps" —to form the "Ascending Complement," partly but not exactly balanced by a "descending Complement" of the sick, crippled, and those traveling. None of these groups, nor the groups comprising the male and female "tots," nor the "patriarchs," are counted as contributing toward the integral soul. The rest of the inhabitants (cherubs, seraphs, schoolchildren, older schoolchildren, youths, adolescents, grown, Regency [the pivot], athletic, virile, refined, temperate, prudent, reverend, venerable) forming the transitional, ascending, and descending groups, the wings, and the wingtips, are counted, being classed as being either of "full character" or "half character." The 810 full character, 405 half character, plus those who are too young, too old, or too sick to have a character—and the absent—make up the grand total of 1,620.[2]

What this fascinating list does not show is the number and distribution of dominant passions within the Phalanx. Nature, writes Fourier, distributes the passions at random, without any regard for social position. In Civilization this is catastrophic, since for example an "omnitone," or person with seven "spiritual" passions (i.e., the three distributive and four affective ones) could be a lowly shepherd. Civilized education would stifle them, and the shepherd would become antisocial. At the other extreme, Nero was a "tetratone" with four dominant passions: cabalistic, composite, ambition, love; yet again, his own society was unable to accommodate him properly.[3]

The first aim of Harmonian society is thus to recognize and

then to develop characters or temperaments, which is achieved by the science of gastrosophy. Brillat-Savarin's famous aphorism, "tell me what you eat, and I will tell you what you are,"[4] is refined by his distant relative Fourier, who wishes to teach people how to eat (and cook) in order to develop their social potential. The second aim is to ensure, by serial means, that each temperament or character thus developed harmonizes with the others: all are equally necessary and each has its correct place in a very large number of groups. Each Phalanx will contain the following characters or personality types:

DO	Solitones	576,	Any Dominant passion
S, f,	*mixed*	80,	1 spiritual, 1 sensual [passion]
RE	Bitones	96,	2 spiritual
S, f,	*bimixed*	16,	1 spiritual, 2 sensual
MI	Tritones	24,	3 spiritual
FA	Tetratones	8,	4 spiritual
S, f,	*bimixed*	8,	2 spiritual, 3 sensual
SOL	Pentatones	2,	5 spiritual

The letters s and f indicate sharp and flat, the intermediary keys in the musical and passional scales. (VI, 340-41)

There will also be rarer characters, perhaps only one for every forty Phalanxes or more, up to the "omnitones" (ibid., pp. 341-42). Every person will recognize his true place, believes Fourier: a solitone will not wish to be the "character president" of a Phalanx since the the function requires an enormous variety of different tasks (ibid., p. 342). Conversely, nobody will envy the King and Queen of passions, however humble their origins (Fourier might have reminded us at this point that, in Harmony, this is all the more unlikely since virtually everybody is monarch or champion of something).

The passionate series, writes Fourier, is:

a league of different groups arranged in ascending and descending order, brought together through a passionate affinity of taste for a certain function, such as the growing of a fruit. It assigns a special group to each kind of work necessitated by the object it is concerned with. If it is growing hyacinths or potatoes, it must form as many groups as there are varieties of hyacinth that can be cultivated on its land, and likewise for potatoes. (VI, 52)

A series, he continues, must not be isolated, since it would have no properties. It must be "enmeshed" with others, forty-five or fifty at least (ibid., p. 53). Conversely, it must be formed of at least three groups, with seven to nine as a good average (III, 20-21), although the number can be considerably higher (up to thirty-two is mentioned, V, 496), with a consequently better range of "harmonies" and "discords."[5] For to work properly, the series must fulfill at least three conditions in addition to the one mentioned above. First, the affinity of taste (harmony or "accord") must be balanced by all kinds of inequality or "discord": a series is formed of "contrasted and ordered inequalities; it needs as many contrasts and antipathies as harmonies or sympathies, just as in music a chord is formed by excluding as many notes as are used" (VI, 53). The rule to follow is again based on music: each group must be completely antipathetic to its immediate neighbors, less antipathetic to less immediate neighbors, and so on, the degree of antipathy being proportionate to the degree of contiguity, just as "D clashes with C sharp and with E flat" (ibid.).

The second condition is that the center must balance the two extremes, or, as Fourier puts it, "the product of the extremes is equal to the square of the median term" (XII, 439). What is meant in practice is that the tensions within each series are so organized that it does not fall apart. The third condition, which is closely associated with the notion of discord and enables "enmeshing" to occur, is that each end of the series should be transitional. Exceptions or transitions had a vital role to play in Fourier's system, and he never ceased referring to the marvelous transitional or "ambiguous" species with which the world was already blessed: the orang-outang, the quince, the medlar, the nectarine, the bat, and amphibious creatures, to mention only a few. The "rule of seven eighths" (seven eighths harmony and one eighth discord in every domain of movement, VII, 6-7) explains the absolute necessity for exceptions in Harmony, without which the distributive passions—closely associated with the formation of series—would just not work. How could the cabalistic passion function, for instance, if everybody were in agreement all the time (ibid., p. 7)? "Nothing would be linked without the ambigu-

ous" (II, 204), wrote Fourier, indicating once again that the aim
of his complex classifications was to delimit in order better to
associate and that taxonomy and analogy are two aspects of the
same basic operation. The role of the "ambiguous" is particularly
important in the love relationship as Fourier saw it, with tendencies normally considered deviant (notably female homosexuality)
appearing sometimes to form the mainspring of society.

If the series are properly constituted, according to the criteria
outlined, they will satisfy the three distributive passions that are
so harmful in Civilization. The "cabalistic" will have free rein,
thanks to the principle of discord between contiguous groups, and
the "butterfly" will be satisfied by the number and variety of
groups and series, which will necessitate changes of session every
two hours at the most. As for the "composite," it is fostered by
the division of functions, so that each person does exactly what
suits him best, all day long, in a variety of tasks (VI, 54). Instead
of facing a long, boring day doing the same thing, the Harmonian
passes from pleasure to pleasure, with not a minute being lost.

As "work" in Harmony is mainly concerned with agriculture
and horticulture, it is not surprising that Fourier's most famous
illustration of how a series functions should come from one of
these domains:

PEAR-GROWING SERIES

Composed of 32 groups

Divisions	Numerical PROGRESSION	Types cultivated
1. Front Outpost	2 groups	Quinces and hard bastard types.
2. Ascending Wingtip	4 groups	Hard cooking Pears.
3. Ascending Wing	6 groups	Crisp Pears.
4. Center of Series	8 groups	Juicy Pears.
5. Descending Wing	6 groups	Compact Pears.
6. Descending Wingtip	4 groups	Mealy Pears.
7. Rear Outpost	2 groups	Medlars and soft bastard types. (I, 294)

Other examples come mainly from the realm of eating: the nine
groups of sauce-lovers (IV, 393-95) or the connoisseurs of bread,
passionately divided or united according to their individual tastes,

from the most common to the bizarre or transitional. Taking as his example the four varieties in the making of bread: the proportion of yeast, salt, and flour, plus the time of baking, Fourier asserts that the preparation of any food in fifty or sixty different ways will cost even less than one. There are limits, of course, which will be calculated elsewhere . . . (ibid., pp. 397-99).

The serial division of work and play will satisfy the individual and society because it makes use of "compound" motives. In Civilization, the three distributive passions are in permanent conflict (III, 233), and all our desires are "simple": we want to get rich, for instance, without realizing that, if everybody became rich, the desire to have servants could not be fulfilled (ibid.). In Harmony, one's motives are (nearly) always compound, combining the "spiritual" and the "material" (IV, 348-51): ambition and love will frequently work together, for instance, or cupidity and friendship. Out of two men working in an orchard, one may like his work as well as his companion and his companion may only like his work. Their relationship is "hemiphiliac" (!) since there is a double motive for working together on the one hand and only one on the other. If this is not a very powerful relationship, continues Fourier, one should remember that in Civilization the person concerned would be antipathetic (ibid., p. 358). Gastronomy is "compound", becoming gastrosophy, when good cheer and friendship (or love) bring people together at a properly organized table, in place of the chaotic and expensive banquets of Civilization (I, 170). Harmony itself will be "BI-COMPOUND," thanks to the reciprocal conciliation of the interests of the individual and those of society (V, 533).

Perhaps the simplest explanation of what it means to participate in passionate series is given by Fourier as one of seven conditions for "societary work": "They [the tasks] should be carried out by groups of friends who have come together spontaneously thanks to the stimulation and intrigues of very active rivalries."[6] The obvious question is, would it all work? To which there is an obvious answer, in the form of an inspired remark of Jean Goret, which we are obliged to translate by a solecism in order to retain its flavor: "The societary experiment has never been tried *nowhere*" (his italics).[7] There are however two strong and closely related theoretical objections, made many years ago, and extended by more recent critics of Fourier. First, why should it be assumed that the passion for a fruit can be classed in exactly the same way as a fruit is classed? Second, if one likes fish, does one automatically become a fisherman?[8] One possible answer is that the principles upon which the serial organization of work are based need modification in two ways, which might even simplify the final scheme of things. First, series must be divided into producing and consuming kinds, with membership of the one sort not necessarily entailing membership of the other. This simply adds one more factor to those already involved. Second, Fourier's principle of exception (the rule of seven eighths) might be invoked to account for the discrepancy between the possible varieties of a product and the maximum number necessary to please all members of the community. Against this, Fourier would argue that our tastes will be developed in Harmony and that we will become more discerning and finicky. Moreover, our first proposal runs counter to the author's analogical beliefs. Perhaps a reorganization of animal, vegetable, and mineral species in accordance with our desires would overcome this difficulty: Fourier's inventiveness would clearly be up to it, and it would be a splendid example of mankind's ability to intervene in the scheme of things.

II   *Work and Remuneration*

The administrative apparatus of a Phalanx is very light, since work-groups are freely formed, by mutual consent or attraction. At the same time, the daily self-organization of some 1,600 people, most of whom belong to up to fifty different work-groups necessitating changes every ninety minutes or so, is a daunting prospect. Fourier nicely combines parody and the creation of a few jobs for functionaries in his invention of the "Work Exchange," the detail of which is largely relegated to his unpublished manuscripts. Briefly, a number of "work-brokers" can, by means of signs, negotiate on behalf of a large number of clients who are involved in as many as thirty "intrigues" at once. The whole is a kind of apotheosis of the cabalistic spirit:

Each day, in each canton, at least eight hundred collective work sessions, meal times, love intrigues, journeys, and other matters are negotiated. As each meeting involves ten, twenty, sometimes even one hundred people, there are at least twenty thousand intrigues an hour to sort out. In order to resolve them, there are all kinds of officials . . . and the Exchange of the smallest canton is thus busier than that of London or Amsterdam. (I, 171-72)[9]

The Harmonian's day is a long one, since he sleeps very little, the prospect of another round of pleasures and intrigues getting everybody up at the crack of dawn—even if his bed has been shared by the most congenial of companions (V, 536). The day is filled by work, eating, and erotic activities, the enumeration of which fails to do justice to their close association. Even the poorest man in Harmony has a timetable full of enough interest to last a rich man in Civilization an entire year. We thus meet Lucas again, and read his timetable for a June day. He gets up at 3:30, has work sessions in the stables and gardens before breakfasting at 7:00, after which he successively reaps, has a session under a tent with fellow vegetable-growers, and goes to the barnyard. At 1:00 he lunches, followed by participation in another three work groups and the "Work Exchange" before supper at 8:30. An hour's social intercourse follows, followed by bed at 10:00. Fourier adds an apologetic note to the timetable explaining that Lucas only eats three meals a day because he lives in the early stages of Harmony. Later on, everyone will have prodigious appetites, which five meals will barely satisfy (VI, 67-68). The timetable of a rich Harmonian, Mondor, illustrates better the delights in store:

MONDOR'S DAY IN SUMMER

Time	
	Sleep from 10:30 at night to 3:00 in the morning
3:30	Rising, preparations.
4:00	Rising court ["cour de lever"], the night's intrigues recounted.
4:30	*Rising-meal* ["délité"]: first meal, followed by work parade.
5:30	Session with the hunting group.
7:00	Fishing-group.
8:00	Lunch, newspapers.
9:00	Session with the horticulture group, under a tent.
10:00	Mass.
10:30	Pheasant-breeders group.
11:30	Library
1:00	DINNER.
2:30	Greenhouse group.

4:00	Exotic plants group.
5:00	Fishbreeders group.
6:00	*Snack* in the fields.
6:30	Merino sheep group.
8:00	Work-Exchange.
9:00	SUPPER, fifth meal.
9:30	Artistic activities [?"cour des arts"], concert, ball, theater, receptions.
10:30	*Bed.*[10]

It is clear from these timetables that, in Harmony as on *Animal Farm*, some are more equal than others. Fourier vigorously defended the principle of inequality, since it is a concomitant of contrast (XIb, 53), although he also maintained the principle of a decent minimum for all. Gross inequalities in Harmony are prevented by the yearly payment of dividends, calculated according to the Harmonian's "input" of capital, work, and talent. Although Fourier's calculations vary, these are normally allotted 4/12, 5/12, and 3/12 of the total respectively. But as an individual belongs to perhaps thirty series and one hundred groups, which may be more or less efficient,[11] how is his dividend calculated? First, the initial dividend is given to each series, and does not depend on their productivity, but on the combined productivity of all series. Second, the proportion the series receives is modified according to its necessity, utility, or attractiveness. For instance, orchard-growers' series receive less than horticulture series because, although they might be more productive and more attractive—efforts may even have to be made to reduce their recruiting power—they are in fact less useful than the latter. The horticulture series, although relatively unattractive, is of crucial educational importance for females and children, who pass from it to the study of agronomy. Its utility is therefore very high. For similar reasons, Opera will be classed as a "second order necessary series," immediately after the first order, which includes latrine-cleaning, looking after babies, and tripe preparation. To prevent greedy Harmonians from indulging simultaneously in latrine-cleaning, rearing of infants, operatic performances and flower-growing, Fourier skillfully uses other factors, including the number of series frequented and the duration of work sessions, to ensure justice—but not equality—for everybody (VI, 303-23).

III   *Agriculture, Gastrosophy, and Love*

Harmony's economy is basically agricultural, in accordance with the wishes of God (VIII, 350). Work in factories is only one quarter as attractive as work on the land, and it would be senseless to increase industrial productivity (VI, 151-53). The Phalanx's economy is characterized by relative restriction in manufactured goods and a superabundance of food. On the one hand, Fourier calculates how the economizing of matches, pins, and the like can save the world four hundred thousand million francs per annum (IV, 208); on the other, the only calamity in Harmony will be a superfluity of foodstuffs, which can be overcome thanks to the good offices of "positive nutritionists," whose role it is to develop our voracity (VII, 138).

In the delightfully simple economy of Harmony, food is produced to match our prodigious appetites, and our appetites stimulated to keep pace with the development of agriculture. Eating, or Gastrosophy—the art of "compound" eating—is one of the three principal activities on the Phalanx, occasionally seeming the most important of all. Its theoretical justifications are many and varied:[12] it is a major means of enmeshing series (VI, 253), a source of "cabalistic refinement" for women (ibid., 256), a vital element in education (V, 76 and *passim*) and a stimulant for all the passions (VI, 261-64). With medicine, it combines to form a new science, the "medicine of taste" or theory of pleasant remedies for every illness (ibid., p. 260).

Such an important activity merits a kind of state policy, which Fourier outlines in yet another passage combining parody and poetic fantasy. The first rule is that quality should take precedence over quantity: Harmonian man may eat a prodigious amount, but it is spread over five meals and four "interludes," for the appetite must never become jaded through excess: continuity of gastronomic (and sexual) pleasure is far more important than paroxysms:

. . . we must take pains to consume a great deal, we must stimulate and maintain appetites among people of all ages. If this condition is not fulfilled, the products of our work will be scorned and will have to be thrown down the drains. Series will become tired of their work when they see its fruits disdained. Hence we see that the key to wisdom and social

policy is the art of keeping mankind's appetite up for his nine meals.
(VII, 133-34)

To this end, each meal must be so composed as to accelerate
digestion in time for the next one, which will follow after a ninety-
minute interval. Our digestion will be further helped by carefully
organized entertainment during the meal. The whole gastronomic
policy will be decided by a series of debates on a massive scale,
culminating in an Ecumenical Council, at which certain sects may
even present heretical theses, just as the Albigenses did in France
or the Hussites in Bohemia (ibid., 134-44).

The "debates" over which the Council presides are unusual in
that they take the form of peaceful wars, which Fourier invents in
order to divert mankind's aggressive instincts into useful channels.
Each Phalanx sends males and females to do gastronomic battle in
the "industrial" or work armies which roam the globe, participating, for example, in the World War of Meat Pies.[13] Enormous
armies make peaceful war . . . and love, for days on end, after
which the Council deliberates and pronounces its judgment. The
inhabitant of a Phalanx thus spends not only many hours a day
eating, but frequent periods away in various armies whose basic
concern is the wellbeing of his stomach. Fourier recounts how a
man in Lyons used to eat entire turkeys, half a dozen chickens
complete with feathers, and whole sides of lamb. "The colossal
appetite of this man is a crudely precise image of [the appetite]
with which gastrosophic education will endow Harmonians," he
writes (V, 137), endowing them a little later with an ostrich's
stomach (ibid., p. 144).

Passages such as this demonstrate very clearly the circular
nature of the Phalanx's economy, to which the composition of the
series also attests: the consumer is *automatically* a producer of the
same commodity. What circulates is food: economically and
above all, physiologically, for behind the detailed description of
the endless, and eventually mountainous, meals, there lies a
matriarchal (as opposed to a patriarchal) society, the image of the
Mother who dispenses *oral* satisfaction.[14] The Phalanstery's
sexual economy is restricted, as far as production is concerned,
for in Harmony most women will be sterile.[15] Fourier's interest in
what might be called "nonproductive" forms of sex (male and
female homosexuality) is partly compensated for, we believe, by

his interest in food, the more so as eating is associated not only with the Mother-figure but also, in a general sense, with copulation. He is most explicit on this point in the *Nouveau Monde amoureux*, quoting Sanctorius's remark that "moderate love-making gladdens the soul and helps the digestion" (VII, 135).

It is therefore not surprising that the vast gastronomic battles that occur overlap with wars or crusades whose main object is amorous dalliance. The "Battle of the Meat Pies" is followed immediately by, or to be more exact, merges into a crusade of pious oriental cobblers (VII, 361-76), which is no more than a massive but carefully controlled orgy, accompanied by oceans of sparkling wine and tons of meat pie.[16] The aim—or pretext—of the expedition is to atone for the bloody crusades of past history by taking on massive and repugnant tasks such as cleaning out kitchens or drains in areas where this has been neglected (an unlikely prospect in Harmony). Many of the participants have belonged to the "Little Hordes" in their youth, having acquired there an excellent grounding in such activities.[17] The problem of drudgery is therefore solved by Fourier, whose genial reasoning could be summed up as follows: who would not clean out a sewer, when guaranteed unlimited wine, meat pies, and sex? For when the day's "work" is over, the rewards are swift:

Surprise was great among the mothers and fathers of the Synod when they found, as if by magic, people of corresponding temperament among the body of Odalisks. . . . Urgèle [the Great Pontiff of the Crusade] had, through the offices of an emissary, procured in advance the list of the amorous idiosyncracies of the Synod and had selected his Odalisks accordingly, so that thirty fathers of the passive flagellant sect found thirty Odalisks of the active flagellant sect, and so on. In a few seconds all the armies were matched as if by magic. . . . (VII, 371-72)

IV   *A Space for Encounters*

If we seem to have wandered away from the Phalanx, it has only been in the wake of its inhabitants, who spend a great deal of time traveling (or, to be more correct, no time at all, since they are always depicted as arriving).[18] The picture we have given of life on—or off—the Phalanx draws essentially on two sources: the detailed "official" descriptions, announced as such, in the works published before Fourier's death, and the *Nouveau Monde amoureux*. It is thus a composite one, which emphasizes aspects—love and gastronomy—which play a more restricted part in the versions published during Fourier's lifetime. Without them, a description of the Phalanstery's architecture, and the disposition of the space surrounding it, becomes, we believe, almost meaningless. For the "internal" and "external" space of the Phalanx is designed with one purpose in mind: to facilitate movement and, in particular, "industrial" and erotic encounters. In Harmony, the Phalanx becomes a rather special kind of focal point, one of departure and arrival, part of a *network* of similar points.[19] As Michel Butor writes, in quite another context, "Human space is by no means Euclidean space, whose parts are mutually exclusive. Every place is the focal point of a horizon of other places, the point of origin of a whole series of possible journeys passing through other more or less determined regions."[20] Just as certain elements of Fourier's universe are linked in a kind of *linguistic* democracy by the practice of analogy (all are equally important),[21] others are related in a kind of *geographical* democracy. Whether these analogies of analogies imply a universal sameness, remains to be seen.

Fourier has left us fairly detailed descriptions of the main buildings of the Phalanx, the Phalanstery, including an outline plan (VI, insert between pp. 122-23). Private rooms are unimportant, since the inhabitants are always in the "Seristeries" or public halls, the workshops, the countryside, or the stables; the richest people will only have three rooms (IV, 539). The relationship between private apartments is, however, of the utmost importance. It must of course be effected serially, so as to avoid separating the rich and the poor; on the contrary, their *association* must be fostered by a system of rent fixing, on a "compound" scale. For example, the rents in a wing of the Phalanstery must be arranged as follows: "250, 400, 300, 450, 350, 500, 400, 550, 450, 600, 500, 650. Simple progression . . . would damage self-esteem and inhibit various agents of harmony. It would bring together in the center the rich class, and at the ends, the unimportant. As a result, the ends would be discredited and thought as inferior. One must distinguish the classes, but not isolate them" (VI, 127).

Covered ways are essential in Harmony, since everybody is always on the move from one work-group to another (ibid., pp.

125-26). The most important "room" in the Phalanstery is the "street gallery," which will be continuous on the first floor, permitting easy communication, away from the cold and wet, compared with the draughty palaces of Civilization. The street gallery is connected to a series of underground passages enabling the Harmonian to travel from the main building to outbuildings (IV, 463). Once he leaves the Phalanx. he will have to travel above ground, but transport between Phalanxes is free (ibid., p. 38) and travel encouraged, from the massive crusades or the smaller "passionate caravans" traveling from place to place (Xa, 169-74) to the individual, who knows that he will be welcomed in any one of the globe's five hundred thousand Phalansteries (ibid., p. 39). Main roads are a "salon of unity," maintained by the wandering Little Hordes who keep them in excellent order (V, 149). The final, important stimulant to travel is provided by the "measured potential series," comprising up to 135 groups, which must be formed from a number of Phalanxes: "In this respect it [the potential series] acts as a natural link between different regions. . . . Thus the potential series . . . establishes *natural* work relationships between the different nations and, consequently, passional links . . ." (ibid., p. 319, Fourier's italics).

Rural space around the Phalanx is similarly designed so as to facilitate work relationships between the various series. A long section in the *Théorie de l'unité universelle* (IV, 478-504) compares agriculture on the Phalanx with current practice in Europe and elsewhere. Fourier distinguishes three kinds of agriculture: "simple or massive," "ambiguous or vague," "compound or enmeshed." The first, practiced in France, "excludes interweaving": one has woods here, fields there, and good land is lost to cultivation. The second, writes Fourier, with his usual Anglo- and Sino-phobia,[22] is found in England and China, being characterized by the random mixing of everything on a tiny scale. The third, which will be practised by the Phalanx, is opposed to the civilized system, "where everyone tends to enclose himself" for fear of theft. It will involve the intermingling of all kinds of crops, according to the serial method of distribution, so that not only is the result pleasing aesthetically, it also helps the intermingling of passions. In one of his little *tableaux*, Fourier shows us a group of cherry-growers having a meeting with (I) a group from the neighboring Phalanx, (II) a group of lady dahlia and mallow growers, (III) a group of vegetable growers, and (IV) a group of maidens growing strawberries (ibid., 484). This scene illustrates the cabalistic and composite passions, explains Fourier, since friendly group rivalry is encouraged, and the relationships formed are the product of both cupidity and friendship or love. The passage ends with an amusing attack on the eighteenth-century French poet Delille, who was famous for his depiction of idealized rustic life. On the contrary, writes Fourier, the life of the civilized farm laborer is a round of misery, and civilized agriculture a mass of contradictions (ibid., pp. 499-500).

V *The Course of Pleasure*

Fourier's dislike of enclosed space has already been met, in his essay on "Combined Architecture" (XII, 683-717), in which he makes a plea for the careful planning of urban space so that the eye shall not be arrested by brick walls. The "Trial Phalanx" thus caused the optimistic Fourier certain difficulties, since he foresaw the need to control the continual influx of paying visitors by some kind of enclosure. He overcame the problem by proposing a wall of *railings*, "because Harmonian society does not permit monastic walls, which block the view and transform public thoroughfares into prisons" (VI, 118). In order to facilitate visits, the Trial Phalanx must also be placed near a large town (ibid., p. 117). In this respect, it is quite unlike the usual Utopian community, which is kept as separate as possible from the surrounding world. Fourier was both laudatory and critical of the Paraguayan dictator Rodriguez Francia (1756-1840) who brought about renewal of his country's economy. The praise went to the man who, without knowing it, had applied many of the principles of Association; on the other hand, his methods were "simple" (as opposed to "compound"): failing to see the advantages of communication, "*he created a desert around his realm*" (VIII, 380, Fourier's italics). Although practical reasons are obviously responsible for Fourier's insistence on the non-isolation of his trial community, they confirm what we have already seen: the Phalanx is "open," in terms of its architecture and of its urban and rural space. Within it and outside of it, people travel and meet, thanks to its disposition and to its relationship with other communities.

The travel, we have noted, is never described, the Harmonian departing or, more usually, arriving, which has the effect of annulling the distance between places. Fourier reintroduces the notion of distance, associating it with pleasure and encounters, in his description of the "parcours", a nicely polyvalent word used to qualify the height of satisfaction achieved in Harmony. The "parcours" ("distance covered, route, course, path, circuit, run, trip") is

the amalgam of a number of pleasures enjoyed successively in a short session, linked with skill, each one heightening the other, following one another at such short intervals that one merely glides over each one [a description of various happy events follows]. . . . All of these pleasures, in the course of one hour, compose a course ["parcours"] which must cover ["rouler sur"] *a basic pleasure continuing throughout the session* [Fourier's italics].[23]

Of the seven separate pleasures listed as constituting a typical "parcours", three are actual encounters of various kinds: meeting a friend thought to be dead; making the acquaintance of a famous literary figure; having dinner next to a powerful man who can help one (IV, 188). Apart from being evidence of what Fourier regarded as pleasure—something continuous rather than violent—the "parcours" sheds confirmatory light on his conception of the "place." For the pleasures all occur "in the same building" (ibid.), while being seen as constituting a kind of journey. The journey is essentially temporal, but the terminology used implies movement through space. In their alliance of the focal point and the journey, the concept of the "parcours" and the "road-salon" are a reply to the "thoroughfare-prison," and correspond to the opening or democratization of Utopian space by Fourier, who designs it, not to separate people, but in order to bring them together. Moreover, they are brought together in thousands of places instead of the one "Ideal City." Fourier's insistence on the importance of migration in Harmony (III, 371) is an indication that it will be an era of expansion, perhaps even proliferation. As our sixth chapter will show, Fourier's imagination is not content with populating the globe, since beyond it there lies extra-terrestrial space. . . .

CHAPTER 5

An Integrated Society

I *The Excluded*

THE "decent minimum," which all Harmonians enjoyed, was not just an "industrial" right. Men, women, and children of all classes were entitled to a social minimum, in the widest sense of that term, brought about by the serial organization of work and pleasure. If one single person were not accommodated in terms of a decent living standard and full satisfaction of his passions, then the whole system would have failed. Conversely, Fourier's analysis of Civilization underlines the ways in which it excludes all kinds of people from its doubtful benefits. Among them are the young, the old, the female, the eccentric, and the morally or sexually "perverted." The great merit of Fourier's design for Harmonian living is to find a place for them all.

In Civilization, the young are excluded by education, in that it does its best to stifle their naturally good instincts and treats them as useless and unproductive when they could be already fulfilling a useful role in society. It fills their heads with abstractions for several hours a day, aided by endless sanctions (VI, 218-21); it tries to inculcate virtue and ends up by teaching vice; it is dispensed by fathers whose only aim is to instill a love of money into their children; or it is dispensed by classmates and servants, who work against the fathers (V, 202-203). Then, at the age of sixteen, a kind of rupture occurs and education starts all over again, with the child's *integration* now at stake. He is taught to laugh at moral dogmas, to exercise hypocrisy, and to lead a generally depraved life so that he can enter adult society fully conversant with its vices (ibid., pp. 203-204). In short, education in Civilization is in contradiction with itself, and contrary to nature (VI, 169), whereas in Harmony, its main aim is the full development of the child's passions and interests. At the other end of the spectrum of age, the old are excluded with equal hypocrisy: everybody

76

pretends to love them, but in fact they are kept apart and mocked secretly, or sometimes quite openly (XIb, 230).

But the most painful form of exclusion is moral and sexual, affecting the old, the "perverted," and particularly women. "In civilized society," writes Fourier, "old age allows *neither men nor women* any chance in love" (V, 226, his italics). Their isolation is neither *natural* nor *real* (Fourier's italics): those men who can afford the expense buy the favors of a few young girls while pretending that they have given up sexually; and no sovereign, however old, ever renounced his seraglio. Those who do give up simply haven't the money to pay (ibid.). Fourier thus credits all male senior citizens with a sexual appetite equal to Victor Hugo's in his late life, since it was inconceivable to him that desire might diminish with age: an exaggeration, but one born of a feeling for fellow outcasts. He was well into middle age when he wrote these lines, living in self-imposed exile in the country. Characteristically, the form of exclusion which civilized society exercises in respect of the pervert or the eccentric is consistently described as *mockery* (VII, 335) and the defense, *dissimulation* (ibid., p. 394). Fourier talks of his own secret "mania," "saphienism," or the wish to further the desires of lesbians (ibid., p. 389). In Harmony, it will have its place, along with the desires of the lesbians themselves, all manner of other "manias," and the activities of socially integrated Neros and Sades. Finally, women, whether "deviant" or not, whom Civilization equates with Negroes (VI, 201) will in theory be on an equal social and sexual footing with men in Harmony, exercising various professions and having an important sacerdotal role. This, as we shall see, leads Fourier and his commentators into some tight corners.

II   *Education*

It is said that Fourier disliked children. If it is true, then the educational policy outlined at length in two of his published works (the *Théorie de l'unité universelle* and the *Nouveau Monde industriel et sociétaire*) is probably yet another part of the immense edifice of wish-fulfillment constructed by his writings. Fourier's notion of education also reverses the relationship between individual and society that usually pertains in Utopia, where pedagogy has an important place: given the careful organization

of society, the individual must be carefully taught how to "fit in."[1]
Conversely, for Harmonian society to function properly, the
individual's aspirations and desires, *however bizarre*, must be
allowed free rein. In spite of this, Fourier's views on education
have been treated with respect in the Soviet Union for many years.
They also anticipate numerous enlightened practices elsewhere,
notably those at Summerhill in England.[2]

The usual principles are invoked at the outset of Fourier's
discussions of education. It must be "integral" and "compound," forming the body and the soul; it is "moral" and "political," since its aim is unity. For this reason, it must foster from
the earliest age the instinctive vocations (in the plural) for which
nature destines us (V, 2-3). Fourier stresses that unity does not
imply equality of wealth (ibid., p. 5), since one of the pleasures of
Harmony is encountering people of different social classes. As
luxury is the first "source of attraction" (ibid., p. 3), education
must also have a productive aim. We can already sense the special
flavor of Harmonian education: it will concentrate on the physical[3] rather than the intellectual, and it is utilitarian in a rather
special way, thanks to Fourier's belief that work is pleasure.

Fourier divides childhood into various phases, which are
roughly as follows (the detail varies): from birth to two ("prime
infancy"); from two to four and a half ("early childhood"); from
four and a half to nine ("middle childhood"); from nine to fifteen and a half ("late childhood"); from fifteen and a half to
twenty ("mixed childhood," or adolescence: [VI, 170]). Until the
age of nine, the "material" aspect will be emphasized, and from
twelve upwards, the "spiritual" (V, 8). The divisions are not
rigid, although Fourier accounts for the precocious child rather
better than the backward one, since progression from one class or
"choir" to a higher one is achieved by the satisfactory completion
of various physical and intellectual exercises (ibid., pp. 9-10).
Children who fail to complete them satisfactorily may repeat for
up to six months, until they either pass or are relegated to the
"half-character" choirs, whereupon parents "cannot deceive
themselves about their inferiority, nor extol the virtues of a little
blockhead" (ibid., p. 23). Much later in the same volume, Fourier
makes a half-hearted attempt at correcting the harshness of this
by claiming that analogical study, which can only be begun at the
age of fifteen, may enable later developers to blossom (ibid., p.

304). It is clear that the backward child, even though he is classed as transitional or "ambiguous" (ibid.) interested him far less than many other inhabitants of this important category. Fourier's interest in the socially strange or deviant does him credit, but it is indulged in at the expense of the very dull or the retarded. On the other hand, what we would call the "mediocre" are catered for rather better by Fourier's insistence on the vocational nature of education.

From their birth, children are separated according to the amount of noise they make, and housed in "séristeries" or crèches, where they are looked after by nursemaids. Their natural parents have other, productive, things to do. Nursing, like all functions in Harmony, is part-time, and only concerns those women who enjoy it (one in four, Fourier calculates). From the age of six months, the child's manual dexterity will be developed, along with his composite and butterfly passions. A special bed, consisting of an elastic base, and sides separating him from his companions, stimulates the composite through the encouragement of movement and the striving for social contact. The butterfly is developed by continually moving the child from his cradle to the elastic bed and back, and by varying his sensory pleasures, in particular the alimentary and visual. The cabalistic spirit does not exist yet, claims Fourier, since the child cannot talk! (VI, 170-80).

From the age of two and a half, children should be encouraged to develop their vocational instincts, up to thirty, whereas in Civilization they barely manage one by the time they reach adulthood (V, 19). It is a lie, maintains Fourier, to proclaim that children are naturally lazy. The reverse is true, and the Phalanx, with its diverse work series, is an ideal place for them to exercise their five dominant characteristics: rummaging, noise, imitation, love of small things, and desire to be led by elder children (VI, 181). The child of two will therefore be taken along to miniature workshops where his three-year-old friends are already wielding hammers and the like. He is too young for this, but a trivial task can be found for him. The important thing is less his productivity, which will be virtually nil, than the development in him of a cooperative and emulative spirit. Fourier describes how children aged two or three can be put to work sorting peas, with the youngest collecting the biggest. As his dexterity grows, he deals with smaller ones until one day he will be solemnly presented with the pompon of "candidate for the group of green pea shellers" (ibid., 182-83).

A little later, in one of his fictional anecdotes, Fourier relates how initial failure can be followed by success. Nisus and Euryale, three-year-olds interested in gardening, are taken one morning by their male nurse, Hilarion, to meet some slightly older children who are gathering vegetables. Two of their friends belong to this group. They want to help, but fail miserably at the trial tasks they are given and are sent away in disgrace. Hilarion gives them toys on which to practice, and after three days they perform well enough to be admitted as candidates for membership of the group. Toys can—and should—always be instructive, comments Fourier (ibid., pp. 193-94).

Between the ages of three and four and a half, the child's character and temperament should become apparent, and its "industrial" capacity should develop. It is therefore a crucial period for both child and Phalanx, which assigns male and female "mentors" to the task of developing all the child's desires, and of deciding whether the infant should belong to the "full" or "half" character choir. Fourier is never very explicit about what constitutes a "half" character, and admission of a child to each choir seems ultimately to depend on the children already constituting it rather than the body of mentors (ibid., p. 198). He claims that membership of a "half character" choir, although hardly flattering, is not a disgrace, since it contains some intelligent people, and also some "precious," ambiguous ones (ibid.). Nevertheless, his educational policy still appears rather more elitist than he would like us to believe. The balance is somewhat redressed by Fourier's insistence that no distinction in dress should be made between the sexes at this age, since completely free development of vocational instincts must be allowed. Difference in dress might prevent this, and it is imperative that neither sex should be excluded from any function (ibid., p. 191).

Fourier named children from four and a half to nine "Cherubims" and "Seraphims." Admission to their ranks was, as usual, by examination. A female candidate would, for instance, have to: display musical and choreographical talent; wash 120 plates in half an hour without breaking any; peel half a hundredweight of apples in a fixed time; sort rice or grain in a fixed time; light and extinguish fire promptly and intelligently (ibid., p. 196). Having survived this, she—and her male counterpart—would then spend a great deal of the next four years or so participating in operatic performances and learning how to cook.

Opera and cooking are for Fourier two of the most important educational activities for this age group, developing children's two active senses (taste and smell: cooking) and their two passive ones (sight and hearing: opera).[4] Harmonian education is based on the belief that a child's body is the coadjutor of his soul: "It considers the soul like a great lord, who arrives at his castle only after his steward has prepared the way" (V, 75). The material stage of a child's development is therefore perfected by these two arts, in which he *participates*: performing in opera, and preparing food as well as eating it. We meet again the short-circuiting of the traditional producer to intermediary to consumer arrangement, which in the case of opera is dispensed with by the transformation of the spectator into an actor. "There will be no actors when everybody is one," writes Fourier, equating acting in Civilization with falsity, and in Harmony with truth (ibid., pp. 78-79).

All branches of material unity are represented in the opera, forming a scale:

K. *Measured participation, by all sexes and ages.*
1. *Song* or measured human voice.
2. *Instruments* or measured artificial sound.
3. *Poetry* or measured words.
4. *Gesture* or measured expression.
5. *Dance* or measured steps.
6. *Gymnastics* or measured movement.
7. *Painting* or measured costumes and designs.
✕ TECHNIQUE or *measured geometric distribution.*
Opera is thus the combination of all material harmonies. . . and the active emblem of the spirit of God, or spirit of measured unity. (ibid., p. 77)

If the child masters these, he will quickly pass on to the spiritual unities, comments Fourier (ibid., p. 78). Parents need not worry about their daughters being perverted by theatrical activities, as is the case in Civilization. In Harmony the "social mechanism" is such as to protect young girls in any situation (ibid., pp. 79-80). From this reassuring statement Fourier passes on to the general importance of opera as a *pathway* to social harmony (ibid., pp. 82-84). The metaphor is interesting, since it is another example of the qualification of the topical in terms of movement or space.

The notion receives a nonmetaphorical corollary when we read elsewhere that the existence of operas in every Phalanx will be a major stimulant to travel (I, 157-58).

The main aim of culinary education is to refine the child's natural gluttony until it becomes what Fourier calls "gourmandise," which is synonymous, he claims, with "gastronomy"; by teaching the child how to cook, society will develop his taste. This is of crucial importance "industrially," since a knowledge of the relationship between culinary and agricultural management is an essential basis for the proper cultivation of vegetables or the raising of stock. In the future, agricultural groups will grow vegetables and feed animals in accordance with what they know about the exigencies of culinary preparation. In this way, cooking becomes a vital part of agricultural studies (V, 102-104). It is also an excellent means of developing the child's cabalistic instinct and thereby preparing him for membership of groups and series. So from an early age he is encouraged to be what we would call "finicky," distinguishing between and liking (or disliking) all manner of foodstuffs and all kinds of ways of preparing them (ibid., pp. 104-105). When he has become adept at growing, preserving, and cooking, he will become a gastronome, ready to take up the science of "compound hygiene," or the application of gourmandise to the 810 temperaments (ibid., pp. 105-107).[5] Special kitchens will be built for him, with miniature cooking utensils; to the attractiveness of working in such an environment will be added the charm of direct and indirect rivalry and the glory of various offices, creating the kind of "hyper-compound attraction" typical of Harmonian life (ibid., pp. 109-15).

By the age of nine, the Harmonian child will have developed his corporal or material faculties to a high degree. It is now time to concentrate on his moral development and encourage his feelings of friendship, honor, and patriotism. Intellectual development will be deferred (ibid., pp. 131-33), along with sexual awareness (ibid., p. 135): one should remember that, for Fourier, children formed a third or "neuter" sex (III, 168). This will not be difficult, as in Harmony the regular practice of gymnastics will retard puberty until the age of nineteen or twenty (V, 195). We shall return to this unconvincing assertion a little later.

Four "corporations" dominate the period from nine to eighteen or nineteen years of age: children are members of the "Little

Hordes" or the "Little Bands" until the age of fifteen or so, after which the body of Vestals will (hopefully) keep sex at bay for a few more years. The "Little Hordes" are one of Fourier's most picturesque inventions, making the "Little Bands" seem rather drab by comparison. Fourier realizes full well that the problem of drudgery will be an acute one in Harmony. As unlimited sex and wine are not available to, or desired by, nine- to fifteen-year-olds, Fourier has to find another form of attraction. This is provided very simply by the object of their labors: filth. For two-thirds of male and one-third of female children of this age-group delight in it (ibid., pp. 143-44). All that is necessary is to form them into corporations and groups according to the kind of dirty task they prefer, dress them up, and turn the whole exercise into a gigantic parody of military maneuvers (ibid., pp. 144-45).

Among the Little Hordes' many tasks are latrine, stable, and sewer cleaning, dung-hill maintenance, road repair, and reptile extermination. They perform very important civic functions and in particular teach, by example, the contempt of money. They are the least remunerated of all the series, and their members are given the right to dispose of one eighth of their earnings to the public purse upon being admitted to membership. At the yearly dividend-paying ceremony, they may donate money to any series complaining that it has been unfairly treated, thereby shaming it into accepting its share without question the following year (ibid., pp. 146-52). Their main salary is public approbation, for they are given places of honor at all ceremonies and are treated with respect, even reverence. When industrial armies are gathered together, the Little Hordes have the right to make the first charge (ibid., pp. 153-54). Their public devotion is possible because to the love of filth are added the two motives of "unitary religious spirit and corporate honor" (ibid., p. 159): their duties, like those of so many other bodies in Harmony, have distinctly religious overtones.

The Little Bands are in every respect diametrically opposed to the Little Hordes, who are noisy and rough. Their specialties are study, cultivation, and manufacture; they dress differently from the Little Hordes and maneuver in a different fashion. Their civic function is to be guardians of "social charm," whereas the Little Hordes maintain "social honor." In place of the general protection of animals which is another function of their rival sect, they care for the vegetable world, including flowers. They also look after bees and silkworms, and watch over linguistic usage. In general, they keep the Phalanx tidy, complementing the road-mending operations of the Little Hordes by more genteel social works, becoming a kind of "physical and spiritual adornment of the whole canton" (VI, 214). The list of their functions is long, but curiously difficult to remember, possibly on account of their triviality. Although Fourier claims that the division of functions between the Little Hordes and the Little Bands demonstrates their equality, the feminine sex thus being the counterweight rather than the valet of the masculine one (V, 182), the social importance of "feminine" tasks is not *depicted* as being as great as "masculine" ones, however strong the theoretical arguments may be. One has the uneasy feeling that Fourier simply allots to the Little Bands anything that is left over after the Little Hordes have gone on their stercoraceous way.[6]

The role of the Vestals is even more difficult to justify, although their functions are clear enough. At the age of sixteen, all children enter the body of Vestals, until they lose their virginity, which is no disgrace in Harmony. They then enter the Damsels' choir. Human nature being what it is, the girls resist longer, so that the sixth "tribe" of the Phalanx is composed as follows: "Vestals (female): 2/6; Vestals (male): 1/6; Damsels (female): 1/6; Damsels (male): 2/6" (ibid., p. 222).[7] The main function of the female Vestals is to satisfy the human need for idolatry, and they have the status of "divine corporation, Shadow of God" (ibid., p. 236). They work with the Little Hordes, whose fostering of the passions of friendship and ambition they complement by their own encouragement of love and familyism (ibid., p. 230). They have an important ceremonial role to perform (ibid., p. 236) and act as a link between classes normally considered incompatible, for instance children and old people, thanks to the admiration they are held in by the former and the respect of the latter (ibid., pp. 239-40). One of the main recompenses for the retention of their virginity (apart from public adulation) is the relatively high chance of marrying a monarch (ibid., pp. 238-39). The male Vestals, being less numerous, have a less important function; indeed, it is not very clear what it is, as Fourier devotes most of his description of this body to a justification of its existence in terms of the advantages accruing to its members (mainly the chance of a rich marriage, ibid., p. 254).

Although the Vestals have important public functions, their main justification lies elsewhere, in their diversionary role. Love, like everything else in Fourier, is codified to a degree, with male and female Damsels, Vestals, Saints, Confessors, Angelic Couples and so on, all of whom have precise roles to perform. But the aim of all of these functionaries except the first two is to facilitate erotic exchange, whereas the Damsels have a neutral role in this respect and the Vestals celebrate its deferment, conserving innocence by their own free will, and thereby set an example to others (ibid., p. 252).[8] It is difficult to avoid the conclusion that Fourier, for all the adult sexual freedom depicted in the *Nouveau Monde amoureux*, was at the very least worried by adolescent sexuality.[9] Significantly, the section preceding the discussion of the vestalate is an attack on sexual morality in Civilization, terminating in rather confused fashion. Harmonian education would be a monstrous failure, asserts Fourier, if, having brought up a child for fifteen years to believe in honor and truth, it then introduced him to a world in which men and women vied in perversity (ibid., p. 220). But as the justification for amorous freedom lies in its dissipation of hypocrisy, it is difficult to accept what is admitted to be a ploy as a basis for sound (and honest) future development. Moreover, the hypothesis is an implicit denial of the unity of Harmony, for if Harmonian education functions so well for the prepubescent child, it *cannot fail* to serve him equally well after this period.

Fourier's description of the course of education ends here, the rest of his exposé concerning the role of teachers, and the choice of teaching methods. The two most important characteristics of the teachers are that they are freely chosen by their students, as in Antiquity, and that they are inevitably part-time, since all work in Harmony is serially organized (ibid., p. 276). Males and females alike become teachers almost automatically, since once they have excelled at one of the many tasks they perform, they are almost certain to attract pupils (ibid., p. 277). In order to explain and classify the teaching methods they may employ, Fourier draws up one of his usual "scales" (ibid., p. 280). The choice of method will depend solely on its suitability to the temperament of the person being taught (and presumably, although Fourier does not say so, of the teacher). Nevertheless, certain basic principles will usually apply, notably that of "beginning locally" (Xb, 251-52): the child will begin studying geography by looking at his immediate neighborhood and history by treating the most recent monarchs (V, 287). The main principle is that of freedom and reciprocity: punishment is unknown, as the recalcitrant child will simply be refused instruction; as teacher and student choose one another, it will therefore be quite common for older children to teach younger ones (ibid., p. 296).

The strengths and weaknesses of Fourier's educational plan are, on the whole, very apparent.[10] His views on the delay of puberty and sex education are absurd. He concentrates on the instincts and the emotions at the expense of the intellect: significantly, nowhere has he anything to say about the choice of syllabus. His account of teaching methods is relatively sketchy and he solves the problem of educational administration by largely avoiding it. The backward and the dull are neglected or treated with condescension, even harshness. On the credit side, there are three or four quite remarkable features. The first, which is easy to overlook, is that Fourier wished to educate women as well as men, and that he wanted to educate them in the same way, with complete equality of opportunity. The second, which largely compensates for—and virtually contradicts—his disparagement of the dull, is the belief, implicit in the serial organization of work (and thus of "apprenticeship") that everyone is good at something. From a very early age, children are encouraged to develop their interests by being taken to all manner of work sessions until they make a free choice of those that appeal to them. This alliance of education in the academic sense and "education for life" meant, for Fourier, education for work, without implying the kind of child labor that was so prevalent at his time. *There are no schools in Harmony.* The tendency nowadays is to integrate the school with the community as a whole by using it for a variety of activities outside normal school hours. Fourier has a similar aim but reverses the process by dispersing the school among the community. The classroom, that focal point of imposed discipline and boredom, disappears and is replaced by the much larger and far more interesting educational arena of the Phalanx itself. Yet again, the open space replaces the closed one. It is this emphasis on integration, the belief that education should form and develop the individual from the beginning as an individual within society, that marks Fourier as a remarkable theorist.

III *The Deviant*

Nowhere in the two long sections we have just been examining does Fourier discuss what is known nowadays as continuing education. He does not, because love, in all its manifestations, is continuing education, whereas education of the young concentrates on other passions. In short, the one complements the other. René Schérer explains the point very well, although in the process he excuses Fourier's vestalic aberrations rather too neatly:

As love, according to Fourier, does not enter man as a radical passion until puberty, it is excluded from the language of education before then, as it cannot lead to practical consequences and would be dangerous verbiage. But in conceiving education as a practical method for developing all the passions apart from love and paternalism (familyism), and in treating the system of love as a kind of education . . . Fourier demonstrates the internal unity of both domains.[11]

Indeed, the excuse tends to limit Fourier too much. For although education of prepubescents may neglect their sexual development, it is nonetheless able to foster their "manias." To illustrate this point, we may turn to yet another of Fourier's little anecdotes. It concerns a little girl who loves garlic and hates reading. In Civilization, we would make her give up her unpleasant habit and concentrate on her studies. In Harmony, instead of recoiling before her ignorance and bad breath, we would give her the "Ode to Garlic" by M. Marcellus and send her off to the garlic-growers' group. In this way, she will be encouraged to read and become a productive member of society through her passionate interest in and defense of garlic growing. "Thus societary education combines the cabalistic spirit and bizarre tastes in order to awaken the study habit in a child," comments Fourier (VI, 257). The role of the mentors, we have seen, is precisely to foster any instinct a child may possess, however odd, while the "major problem" of societary education is "to employ the characters of Nero, Tiberius, Louis XIth, as usefully as those of Titus, Marcus Aurelius, or Henry IVth" (ibid., p. 170).

The deviant, and its recognition, are therefore of crucial importance in Harmony. Fourier defines "manias" or idiosyncrasies as "any fantasy which is judged unreasonable and outside the accepted developments of passion" (VII, 93). Most, but not all, concern the love relationship (love being defined as "the passion of unreason," [ibid., p. 384]), and they range from the relatively common (pederasty; male and female homosexuality), which are practiced in the "whirl" (Phalanx) of Cnidos (ibid., pp. 156-207), to incest (ibid., pp. 250-59), and then a whole range of fascinating minor perversions. Among these are heel-scratching (ibid., p. 334); "prosaphism" or saphienism (ibid., pp. 162, 389); and live spider-eating (ibid., p. 395). The picture is rounded off by sadistic lesbianism (ibid., p. 391). It is a fascinating and amusing gallery, far more varied than the activities described by Sade in *The 120 Days of Sodom*, which are little more than a dreary round of pederasty and coprophagia (one of the activities not described by Fourier).

The story of the sadistic lesbian, Madame Strogonoff, provides Fourier with an excellent opportunity to develop an analysis of what we might call a case history of psychopathology, and is of great interest for the post-Freudian reader:

A Muscovite Princess, Lady Strogonoff, saw she was growing old and became jealous of the beauty of one of her young slaves. She had her tortured and stuck pins into her. What was the real reason for her cruelty? Was it jealousy? No, it was lesbianism. She was an unconscious lesbian, disposed to love her beautiful slave, in whose torture she participated. If someone had put the idea into her head that she was a lesbian and reconciled her and her victim, under these conditions they would have become passionate lovers. But the Princess, unaware of her lesbianism, succumbed to a subversive counter-passion. She persecuted the person with whom she should have enjoyed a pleasurable relationship, and her rage was all the greater because the stifling [of her real passion] was caused by a prejudice that prevented her from seeing its real aim and thus from having even imaginary enjoyment. . . . Others practice in a collective form the atrocities exercised on an individual level by Mme Strogonoff. Nero loved collective or widespread cruelty. Odin made a religious system out of it and Sade a moral system. This taste for atrocities is only the result of the stifling of certain passions. With Nero and Sade it was the composite and butterfly passions that were repressed and with Mme Strogonoff it was a variety of love. (ibid., p. 391)

A clearer example of repression and its disastrous consequences could hardly be given, and the passage shows remarkable insight into the hidden motives of our behavior. Parallels with Freud can, however, be too hasty.[12] Wheras with Freud the person concerned would be subjected to an individual cure, with Fourier the organization of community life would render the repression impossible and a cure therefore superfluous. In Harmony, tension —in the sense of a strained nervous condition—does not exist; the nearest one comes to it is in the lovers' quarrels, which are quickly resolved, the anticipation of pleasure and occasional disappointment, and the friendly rivalries within and between groups. But it could be argued that tension and neuroses are, paradoxically, an indication of the wellbeing of society, since they are a product of its dynamic nature. In creating a social system which prevents them, does not Fourier create a static, unreal society, and in taking care of everybody, does he not run the risk of suppressing individuality—in other words, the reverse of what his system should be doing? The question is a crucial one, and we shall be returning to it when we consider to what extent Harmony is just another Utopia.

IV *The Integration of Women*

The major factor in the integration of women is their education. The description of the activities of the "Little Bands" is followed by a long notice on the "Connivance of the Philosophers and French in the Debasement of the Female Sex," in which Fourier contrasts the fate of women in Civilization with the future they are promised in Harmony: not to serve man, but to vie with him (V, 186-90). The tasks for which they are suited are set out with characteristic precision. In the domain of education, their activities as mentors, as members of the "Little Bands" and of the Body of Vestals, have already been noted. They also perform an important teaching function by virtue of their active participation in various series, where their advice and instruction will be as sought after by novices as those of men (ibid., p. 276).

Women have an almost equal productive role to men, the "productivity-ratio" in Harmony being: "Man: 12; Woman: 9; Child (from 5 to 15): 7. Total: 28" (IX, 538/x). They are particularly suited to certain branches of agriculture, where they will take over "a large part of the minor tasks performed nowadays by men" (V, 100); they will predominate in dressmaking (VI, 190), and in manufacturing work in general they will find certain kinds of tasks more attractive than others. Fourier provides various examples of the division of work according to sex and age:

SPECULATIVE PRIMARY INDUSTRIES

1 for men and male children,	CABINET MAKING	A
2 for women and female children,	PERFUMERY	B
3 for men, women, and children,	CONFECTIONERY	C

SPECULATIVE SECONDARY INDUSTRY FOR THE THREE SEXES

4 *Cheesemaking*	D	5	*Pork Butchery*	E
6 *Preserved Fruit and Vegetables*	F	7	*Seed-Trade*	G

Pivotal ✕ STRINGED INSTRUMENT TRADE.   Ambiguous K BIRD-BREEDING.

(ibid., p. 142)

Another list sets out the proportion of men and women in the arts and sciences, heavy and light agriculture, and various bodies of teachers and baby-minders (ibid., p. 201). The essential, writes Fourier, is that women should occupy half the positions in lucrative tasks while "regaining the position assigned to them by nature, that of rivals and not dependents of man" (ibid., p. 141).

Fourier's division of labor may restore some of woman's lost dignity, but it is effected along very traditional lines, the distribution in arts and sciences giving the men predominance in the latter and the women in the former. We should also remember that the main compensation for retention of virginity in female Vestals is a rich marriage, even if marriage for women in Harmony is exempt from the duplicity characterizing it in Civilization. In other words, Fourier, for all his talk of the freedom which women will enjoy in Harmony, cannot escape from a stereotype in terms of the work they will perform. Their other role is essentially *sacerdotal*, and the problem posed by the emphasis Fourier places on it is whether, on this occasion, the stereotype is deliberately used for parodic effect, or whether he is too bound up in a fantastic or phantasmic world to be able to exercise irony.

The Damsels and Vestals are only two of the many "religious" corporations of the New Amorous World. Bacchantes (male and female), Confessors, Angelic Couples, Saints, Heroes, Pontiffs and others all ensure the smooth running of a society designed to fulfill *every* sexual need. The terminology employed, and the practices described, do seem to indicate a very conscious vein of religious parody, with various elements of Christian ritual being reused. There are, for example, two kinds of Sainthood in Harmony: major or gastronomic, and minor or sexual. Fourier mocks openly the "ridiculous idea of civilized and barbaric people, who reward by the title of saintliness practices that are quite useless to the human race, practices like prayer and asceticism which do nobody any good, not even the person indulging in them" (VII, 119). The devotion of the Angelic Couple is of quite a different kind, their sexual abstinence being in respect of each other for a limited period during which each prostitutes him- or herself to twenty or thirty suitors. This extreme example of philanthropy inspires the greatest admiration and respect on the part of the public (ibid., pp. 78-80, 90-93). Naturally, the tests to be undergone before a person attains such an elevated rank are rigorous. The novice who wishes to achieve the status of Minor Sainthood must undergo seven, including sessions of "prosaphism" or "prohomosexuality," the "satisfaction" of choirs of Reverends and Patriarchs, four sessions of "Angelicate," and so on (ibid., pp. 121-23).

Sainthood is not the prerogative of the female sex, since all the religious bodies described are open to male and female alike, and in the case of the "Angelic Couple" their equal representation is a *sine qua non* of the rank. Nevertheless, the person who is "on stage" longer than anyone else in Fourier (in a dialogue) is female, a "Saintly Heroine" by the name of Fakma, in an episode that is perhaps central to the *Nouveau Monde amoureux*. Through it, Fourier reveals his feelings about the female sex and his own sexual aspirations. It has also been the object of two detailed and very different analyses, by Simone Debout and Catherine Francblin.[13]

The "Arrival of a Band of Knights Errant at the Whirl of Cnidos" (ibid., pp. 156-207) begins just after an advance party of adventurers has been "captured" by the Bacchantes of Cnidos (in Fourier's amorous battles nobody is captured unless they

agree). Various captives are presented in the Reception Hall, with
due courtesy and some preliminary sexual skirmishing, and the
price of their redemption is discussed. Then the news spreads that
the gigantic, beautiful, and saintly sovereign Fakma has been
captured. Various males from the host Phalanx immediately begin
courting her, but in vain. For Fakma, emerging after a month's
exclusive lovemaking with a Khan of Tartary, wants to purify her
soul by an intense "celadonic" passion, or a kind of Platonic
love. The sight of a handsome young seraph, Isaum, who is
currently serving a period as a prosaphist, has aroused feelings of
guilt in her. She is also very tired. . . .

Not surprisingly, none of her male suitors wishes to reciprocate
her feelings, even when she offers to satisfy seven sexually if one
sacrifices himself to a celadonic love for the good of the rest.
They reproach her for her egotism and perversity, to which she
riposts by charges of vulgarity. One is so overcome by emotion
that he faints, whereupon Fakma is accused of the sin of "lèse-
unité," which consists of sacrificing seven people for the happiness of one (herself): the reversal of the principle of "seven-
eighths." Finally, two young lovers, Daphnis and Chloë, offer
themselves to her if she will consent to making all the Cnidians
present happy. Even this is insufficient, and everyone is despairing
when Isaum approaches Fakma and offers her, not twelve hours
of celadonic passion, but a lifetime. This breaks the deadlock, and
the seven guilty Cnidians who had courted her in vain are sen-
tenced to a period of prosaphism. Fakma and Isaum will set themselves up as an "Angelic Couple," and the episode draws near its
close with their joint triumph, amidst scenes of religious fervor,
with the guilty being pardoned so that they can participate in the
sexual festivities. Chrysis, the Great Priest of Cnidos, pronounces
a homily of modern sexual virtue, contrasting it with the subservience of women in Civilization, which has now ceased thanks to
the efforts of "the inventor to whom the earth owes its happiness
today" (ibid., p. 202).

On this self-congratulatory note Fourier closes the scene (fantasy). His commentary (ibid., pp. 203-207) stresses the philanthropic nature of Fakma's future prostitution during her Angelicate, contrasting it with the duplicity to which women are driven
in Civilization. As for the lesbianism which is clearly rife in Harmony, he merely states that one of the many contrasts between the

sexes lies in the penchant of females for homosexuality, which will become almost universal in the harmonian freedom of sexual relationships.

Simone Debout's discussion of this extraordinary episode is detailed, sympathetic, and occasionally lyrical. Like Catherine Francblin — and this is about the only common point in their analyses — she sees Fakma as the Mother Figure, with Isaum as the child (Fourier) who, by his generous action, destroys the ancestral law of the rivalry between Father (the Khan) and children (the suitors): at the end, they are reintegrated, no longer rivals but equal participants in the democracy of universal sexual satisfaction. Fakma's adoption of Isaum is an indication of the "opening" of the family and thus the exorcism of the tensions and taboos (including incest) it normally harbors. Conversely, Isaum may not enjoy his mother, but his action liberates both of them for other sexual unions in which the physical and the sentimental (or celadonic) are allied, while Fakma's saintly prostitution also shows that "the sublime is closely allied to the sensual and [that] any act of communication supposes the revelation of an incomplete being who transcends his limits in joining another body" (Debout, p. 54). Fakma's triumph is a manifestation of feminine independence, and Fourier's description of sacrifice and heroism is a more effective transgression of the ancestral law than revolt. The "pivotal love" of Isaum and Fakma, in its exclusive and disinterested nature, overcomes any jealousy that might exist between mother and son. Finally, the triangle Mother, Son, Father is supplanted by the triangle Mother, Son, God, thanks to the "natural" quality of the mother, who is able to reveal her latent "supernatural" character by virtue of her relationship with her son.

Catherine Francblin implicitly dismisses this as impressionistic nonsense in a pitiless analysis of Fourier's attitude toward women, beginning with various quotations which, she claims, demonstrate that his opinion of the female sex was really very low. Moreover, his practice of classification and the constant appeal to mathematics indicate that his universe, far from being "open," is really "closed," fixed, and therefore incapable of integrating the "flux of the libido" (Francblin, p. 48). Isaum's "sacrifice" is a form of autocastration at the behest of a woman, Fakma, devoid of sexuality: "the symbol of Utopian femininity, a woman indifferent to

the impulses of desire" (p. 51). Fourier's insistence on the natural
lesbianism of women, and passages elsewhere which nevertheless
describe woman's desire for sexual satisfaction by the male, betray
his fear of the feminine sex organ, whose mode of existence is
essentially a "lack" (of the masculine organ), constituting a gap
which must be filled, or sewn up (p. 53). The sacerdotal parapher-
nalia surrounding the cult of celadonic love is one of the many
indications of Fourier's idealism, a Utopian's belief in a transcen-
dental order and in two kinds of nature: a debased "civilized"
one, and a golden Harmonian one. Woman (i.e., Fakma) becomes
a "God-Woman, a phallus-woman" (p. 59), the Mother-figure
who (i) castrates the son, thereby attesting to the Paternal power
invested in her, (ii) is untouchable, but (iii) is simultaneously (ful)-
filled. Fourier's prolesbianism and the lack of homosexuality in
the *New Amorous World* reinforce the phallic nature of the Ideal
Woman, who becomes a manifestation of a new or third "neutral" sex, which abolishes the difference between masculine and
feminine. All tension is thus removed from Harmony, which
thereby affirms its traditional, "fixed," Utopian, character: "A
place without desire, a society without history, such is the terrible
and fascinating gift which Fourier presents us with in the *New
Amorous World*" (p. 69).

If one exempts Fourier from Francblin's charge of slandering
women, since she takes no account of the possible irony of the
passages she quotes, it is difficult not to agree with most of the
main points of her argument. In theory, Fourier's long apology for
celadonic love (VII, 23-115) is justified by the principle of balance: in order to attain spiritual love one must satisfy the exigencies of the flesh (ibid., p. 34). But this is followed by a declaration
of the *superiority* of spiritual love (ibid., p. 62), which leads to the
apotheosis of Fakma and the attendant sacrifice of Isaum. Both
critics acknowledge Fourier's mother-fixation, but the weakness
of Debout's analysis lies in its use of Freud while simultaneously
taking the text at its face value: for instance, Fourier's declaration
that all women are basically lesbian is seen as an indication that he
is redressing the balance, since hitherto homosexuality had been
seen as a largely masculine prerogative. This may or may not be
true, but it appears curiously naïve when read alongside Francblin's analysis.

It is of course possible that we are all taking the episode too seriously. The inflated language, violent emotions, and pseudo-religious setting are an invitation to read it, in part at least, as a hilarious parody: of Courtly Love, and of the theme of the beautiful captive,[14] to take only two possibilities. Fakma, the saintly heroine, defends her virtue against her suitors, who know that it will be a very temporary state, since the defense consists in making one wait while she satisfies the other seven. But the parody need not invalidate the basically psychoanalytical approach of both critics; a purely impressionistic judgment would be that here, as elsewhere in the *Nouveau Monde amoureux*, the author is simultaneously participating in and standing back from his own very private creation. We would therefore conclude neither "for" nor "against" Fourier if he were on trial (which he is in Francblin's essay in particular) for his views on women. His description of their fate in Civilization is acute and persuasive; the allocation of tasks proposed in the less private works is along traditional lines, although various "guarantees" such as job opportunity, are given. On the surface, the elaborate amorous rituals of the *Nouveau Monde amoureux* provide equal sexual opportunity for all. Beneath this democratic surface there may indeed lurk a narcissistic, autoerotic, suppressed homosexual with a mother-fixation.[15] But as long as the expressed *views* are placed in their context and separated from the *motives*, then the debate can profitably continue. As to the question whether Harmony is "fixed" or "open," perhaps we can, like Fourier, defer our discussion just a little longer.

V   *The Old*

Old age is not a very popular subject with writers of fiction, nor indeed with politicians. The former, if they are writing in a traditional vein, probably feel that there is little scope for character development in the old; the latter are unlikely to take much notice of them because they lack industrial bargaining power and are not distributed geographically in a manner likely to alter the course of elections. As a writer of (science-) fiction and the bearer of a sociopolitical message, Fourier might well have neglected the old. But like the young, the deviant, and the female, they are allotted a place in Harmony, where they enjoy the respect due to their social utility.

Once again, the generalized reciprocity of Harmonian life is responsible for their new status, with the "contact of extremes" operating on their behalf in the educational and sexual domains. As instruction is solicited rather than imposed in Harmony, where each series will contain several experts able to undertake part-time teaching, the stock figure of the elderly, mocked teacher gives way to the venerable sage whose advice is eagerly sought (V, 449). The services of the elderly will be presumably even more in demand at the "Court of Love," where they can be employed as male and female "confessors," Fourier's unique version of marriage-counselors. Their role is to match temperamentally hosts and guests in a Phalanx so that complete amorous satisfaction results (VII, 215-16), an immensely complex operation that is detailed in a manner which shows how lunacy can invade even mathematics (XIb, 22-90). One of the fringe benefits of this occupation is that they may end up matching themselves with their clients, for "apart from the fact that many people are drawn to the elderly when they are kind, there will be circumstances under which this penchant will be aroused by the methodical progression of sympathies. A skilful confessoress will manage to discern this need in the soul of her client and will try to awaken it" (VII, 219-20). In case this happy conjuncture does not occur, the sexual needs of the elderly will always be met by the "Angelic Couple", or even the cherubic aspirants to this holy rank, among whose trials are "holocausts" or sessions with the aged of either sex (ibid., pp. 105, 109-10): Isaum, in a supreme gesture of devotion to Fakma, offers his amorous services to all the female Patriarchs of Cnidos (ibid., p. 199).

VI   *A Place for All?*

Not even Fourier can attempt to provide for everyone without some stresses and strains, and certain aspects of his writings on education, the deviant, and women, leave us perplexed and uneasy. In attempting to include those who interested him most—the bizarre—he tends to overlook the dull but numerous, although they are *implicitly* catered for in his educational theories. And are the bizarre always to be integrated as painlessly as Mme Strogonoff? Where women are concerned, the closer Fourier is involved in his own work, the less emancipated they appear. The difficulty with his writings is, yet again, basically linguistic. Either one treats the more private texts as having the same status, as, for instance, the section on education in Fourier's most "public" work, the *Nouveau Monde industriel et sociétaire,* or one attempts to disengage the ironic from the serious and the social discourse from the dream discourse, getting rather lost in the process. Nevertheless, one of the most sensible remarks ever made about Fourier may help us to opt for an ultimately charitable view of his treatment of those we have called the "excluded." After a discussion of the author's masochism, repressed homosexuality, sadism, and paranoia, Frank Manuel notes that, in Fourier's writings, the hatred produces its particular "counterpassion"—the passion produced by the stifling of a dominant passion — whose name is love.[16] For this reason, we are willing to accept Fourier's discussion of the socially excluded on its surface, humane level, and to forget the thwarted passions that frequently inform it.

CHAPTER 6

Fantasy and Cosmology

I *Science Fiction*

THE fabulous maneuvers of amorous armies described in the *Nouveau Monde amoureux* presumably take place in the early days of Harmony. Later on, there will be no need for wine or champagne to celebrate the battle's outcome; instead, the victors can be toasted by dipping one's glass in the ocean. Thanks to changes in the world's climate, a "boreal corona" will be born, which will "change the taste of the seas and decompose or precipitate the bituminous particles through the expansion of a *boreal citric acid.* The fluid, combined with the sea's salt, will give it the taste of a kind of lemonade" (I, 45, Fourier's italics). All Harmonians will eventually be fair, their skins having been bleached by the sun, so that even the black races will become white (Xa, 44): a neat solution to the color problem. Mankind will develop an "archibras" (literally: primitive arm), a kind of gigantic tail, which will serve innumerable purposes:

The [archibras] will enable a man to swim as fast as a fish. . . . A man using it as a support can reach a branch twelve feet high. . . . As soon as one jumps, the [archibras] forms a spiral, at least tripling one's natural velocity. It softens one's fall by two-thirds. It can be made to revolve, conelike, so as to slow down the body, and it can form an inverted parachute by means of which one can fall from a considerable height without risking more than a bruise.[1]

As for Man's sexual activity, it will become contagious, infecting the universe itself. Fourier's "phallic woman"[2] is mirrored in his picture of the universe:

The planets, which are androgynous like plants, copulate with themselves and with the other planets. Thus the earth, by copulating with itself and through the mingling of its two typical aromas [fluids], the masculine,

98

emanating from the north pole, and the feminine, emanating from the south pole, engendered the CHERRY-TREE, subpivotal fruit [tree] of the red fruit [trees]. (IV, 244)

If Fourier's revelations about the sex-life of Harmonians scandalized his disciples, it is not surprising that passages like these — and other writings on metempsychosis, cosmogony, and climatology — confirmed the opinion of many contemporaries that he was mad. Emile Lehouck entitles one section of his intelligent and sympathetic study of Fourier "The Enigma of the Cosmogony,"[3] insisting, as we have done, on the problem posed in the author's work of what can be broadly called the "rational" and the "irrational." What is perplexing is that the many marvels unfolded are described with an apparent seriousness which contrasts with the often mock-heroic accounts of the amorous maneuvers on and off the Phalanx. These marvels should in their turn be taken *seriously*, in the sense that they should not be trivialized by relegation to a kind of museum of Fourier's eccentricities. There are three reasons for this. First, their relegation would also trivialize Fourier's entire system, to which they are as important as the critique of Civilization or the treatises on education. As we have insisted often enough, it must be seen in its *totality*: our natural amusement at the childlike insistence of the writing should not blind us to what the author so often refers to as "the unity of system." Second, they represent, along with the descriptions of the New Amorous World, the most imaginative and poetic part of their author's vast production. Third, all the examples just given, with the exception of the copulation of our planet, might be seen as an imaginative foretaste of developments in biology and climatology that are already being anticipated today. Fourier himself saw no problem, of course, for "everything is simultaneously marvelous and mathematical in social harmony as in the harmony of the universe" (II, 58, second pagination).

Fourier's cosmology and cosmogony also mark the point at which the fiction of Utopia merges into science fiction. The boundary between the two genres is hard to determine, and considerable overlap is virtually inevitable.[4] If Utopia is usually "out of time" (and space), an ideal, highly organized community, while the world of science fiction is a future one in which the impact of science and technology — in all their ramifications — is felt, then that boundary is frequently crossed in Fourier's work. In other words, if the world of the Phalanx is, roughly speaking, a Utopian one, then the passages describing changes in the world's climate, to take one example, are science fiction insofar as they describe, not an ideal society, but natural (future) consequences of that society's existence. When Fourier writes about the building of the Suez and Panama canals (I, 46-47) or the discovery of the North Sea Passage (III, 84-86), his statements are essentially predictions, which may or may not come true: the world of science fiction is sometimes overtaken by reality, which proves or disproves it. Fortunately, the accuracy or otherwise of Fourier's forecasts is secondary to their imaginative coherence.

The improvements just mentioned are a powerful testimony to the influence of mankind on the global and cosmic future. To take one example, the discovery of the North Sea Passage will result from the improvement of the world's climate, which is in turn due to advances in farming techniques, or, as Fourier puts it, the process is one of "atmospheric refinement through the integral cultivation of the globe" (III, 87). The serial system of afforestation will ensure that vines are not destroyed by frost because of uncontrolled felling of trees (ibid., p. 95). The Loire Valley, he writes, lies at the same latitude as Astrakhan or Quebec, but enjoys a far milder climate. Why? Because it is intensely cultivated, whereas the two other places are surrounded by deserts: "Difference in winter cold, 15 or 16 degrees [Réamur], solely because of the lack of cultivation" (ibid., p. 90). If one cultivates widely, practicing the serial or "judicious" distribution of cultivation, then even greater temperature modification can be achieved, 36° in Australia, for instance (ibid., p. 91), while "the vine will ripen on a line from Saint-Petersburg to Stockholm . . . and the orange will grow in the open at Mainz and Paris" (XII, 51).

Such phenomena reinforce Fourier's insistence that the social movement is the "pivotal" one (I, 31), with which the others are coordinated. Humanity's role is thus potentially unlimited. As he wrote in one of his more exalted moments:

Any man who has the ability to found a passional whirl [Phalanx] . . . can work on the temperament of the planet, corrects its aromas, change its temperature and atmosphere, cleanse its seas, stock them with magnificent new species, operate on the aromas of the sun and the various stars, move five of them so that they orbit around our globe, and provide it with two rings like Saturn. (XII, 5)

In other words, the law of the "contact of the extremes" is again in operation, ensuring that the apparently humble can affect that which is most mighty, and reciprocally. If Fourier's cosmos is the product of human — and divine — freewill,[5] with the priority going to humanity, the anthropocentric universe can react to what mankind is up to. As long as mankind behaves itself, by which Fourier means that it is obeying his system, then the universe will function properly. If it is not, then the cosmic disorders and punishments will be on a scale that make Victor Hugo's universe, with its "penal planets,"[6] seem almost modest.

II *An Animistic Universe*

In this way, Fourier's animism extends outside the realm of nature on earth. Beyond our world, stellar and planetary bodies not only react to our affairs; they live, die, copulate, and communicate, by analogy with the destiny of the human race, although the detail of their sex-life transcends our present biology. They are inhabited, not only by beings such as the "Solarians," who are a kind of image of what man will eventually become in Harmony, but also by our souls. For Fourier, Eros is infinitely more important than Thanatos or, to put it more bluntly and unkindly, the unimportance of death in his writings probably betrays his fear of it.

Death, we have seen, plays no real role in Harmony, since it is simply a *transition* to another state, or series of states, which have little to do with the orthodox Christian view of the afterlife. Thanks to a series of rebirths and transmigrations, our souls wander through and populate still further the animistic universe, providing a kind of endless though mute dialogue with the heavenly bodies whose existence both affects and is dependent upon our "mundane" and "transmundane" destiny. There comes a point when the flight of Fourier's cosmological fantasy brings into question the tabular fantasy of man's "social movement" (I, 32, insert). What will happen when the 80,000 years have elapsed? The answer given suggests that the system sometimes transcends itself, thanks to the force of Fourier's imagination: the mathematical is not so much negated by the marvelous as allied to it in the way in which he himself described. Or, as Simone Debout suggests, quoting Fourier, mathematics themselves are "animate(d)" ("animés")[7] in accordance with the dynamism of the universe they are called upon to explain. The system seems closed, if one accepts the finite chronology of the social movement; yet thanks to Fourier's unique cosmogony a whole new dimension is added.

Thus, when Fourier describes man's "transmundane" existence, the end of the animal and vegetable world and the death of the planet tend to be forgotten, or rather, subsumed in an even grander design in which cosmogony (the science of the origins of the universe) and metempsychosis (the transmigration of souls) are inextricably mixed, and the former transformed:

Our cosmogonists no doubt consider that the soul is not part of the Universe, since they give no theory about the past and future destiny of souls that takes account of the destiny of matter. . . . One cannot explain the material destinies of the world without having explained the passional ones. . . . It follows that their [the cosmogonists'] science, which they believed to be simple and confined to the past, comprises six inseparable branches, viz:

SUPERCOMPOUND PSYCHOLOGY or *destiny*

citer-passional,	inter-passional,	and ulter-passional
Past,	present,	future

SUPERCOMPOUND GEOLOGY or *destiny*

citer-material,	inter-material,	and ulter-material
Past,	present,	future (III, 306)

Fourier's "glimpse" of our passional destiny that follows begins by reiterating the principle of the Attractions being proportionate to the Destinies: our life in Civilization is so miserable that the future life, as it is usually described, is relatively uninteresting (ibid., p. 310); something more exciting is needed to satisfy the Harmonians' insatiable appetite for enjoyment (ibid., p. 311). Our metempsychoses must therefore be "compound," and not simple, with our twelve passions being developed to a degree unknown even in Harmony. Fourier calculates that we will have either 810 or 1,620 lives, of which half will be in this world and half elsewhere (ibid., p. 319); of these, 720 will be very happy, 45 reasonably so, and 45 unhappy, since the principle of seven-eighths or seven-ninths will apply here as elsewhere (ibid., p. 320). The happiness of our existences is naturally in accord with the fortunes or misfortunes of our planet, since the human soul and the planetary soul are related. Hence the delay in implementing Harmony hàs already had catastrophic effects on the world's climate (ibid., p. 325). More important still, thanks again to the "unity of the system," when our planet dies "its great soul, and consequently ours that inhere in the great soul, will move to a new globe, a comet. . . . The little souls [i.e. ours] will lose their detailed memory of their metempsychoses and will then merge with and become one with the great soul" (ibid., p. 326). This in its turn will inhabit various planets, gradually moving upwards in the great ladder of creation, becoming the soul of a nebula, of a sun, and eventually of a universe, a "biniverse," a "triniverse," and so on (ibid., p. 327).

Fourier descends (slightly) from these heights to give details of our metempsychoses and the composition of our various bodies: we cannot inhabit animals, since our souls are constructed differently (ibid., p. 329); we cannot remember past existences in this life, although we can in other lives (ibid., p. 330); our souls in other lives take a body "formed by the element we call Aroma, which is incombustible and homogeneous with fire. It penetrates solids readily, as we see from the Aroma called magnetic fluid" (ibid., p. 330);[8] the bodies of "mundanes" are terraqueous, those of the dead are "aromal-ethereal," while those of the "transmundanes" are formed of aroma and air (ibid.) Fourier also reminds us that the transmundanes, like the Harmonians, are not equal (ibid., p. 331), before passing very rapidly over the transition from this life to the next. On the other hand, the transition from another life to life on earth is described precisely: it occurs during teething, before which the infant depends on the great soul of the planet (ibid., p. 335). Finally, the greatest pleasure that is known to the ultramundanes is that of "existing and moving" by flying, a sensation which we sometimes experience while asleep (ibid., pp. 332-33). Students of dreams will have no difficulty in glossing this particular delight. In Civilization we only know the "counterpleasure," writes Fourier: "rest or bed" (ibid., p. 333).

The "material" destiny of the universe, or Fourier's own
version of cosmogony, is treated in detail elsewhere, notably in
the third volume of the *Théorie de l'unité universelle*, in the
Nouveau Monde amoureux, and in two articles entitled, respectively, "Cosmogonie" and "Analogie et cosmogonie" in volume
twelve of the *Œuvres complètes* (pp. 1-34; 35-199). Its great
originality lies not so much in its animism, since Fourier had a
predecessor in Restif de la Bretonne, who also described the
planets' amatory exploits,[9] as in the extension of the notion of
cosmogony to include the modification of the universe by Man's
actions.[10] Fourier endows the earth with five moons: Mercury,
Juno, Ceres, Pallas, Phoebina (or Vesta), plus a "hypo-major
ambiguous" body, Venus (IV, 244).[11] It should have six, but
Phoebe (the Moon) died, causing the Deluge (IV, 244). Their
major function is to supply or create the flora and fauna of the
earth, according to the period of its development. In the one
succeeding Civilization, for instance, "minute agricultural quadrupeds" such as dwarf horses and camels will be created; they
should already exist, but "the planet [earth] was so enfeebled by
the Deluge that she lacked the internal strength necessary for the
rumination and development of the aromas she spilt while copulating [with herself]" (IV, 247).

Our present "estate" is in fact disastrous, since seven-eighths of
the flora and fauna are harmful (ibid., p. 254). However, in
Harmony, all will change:

. . . [the star] who gave us the lion, will give us, in the form of a counter-
mold ["contre-moule"], a superb and docile quadruped, a springy carrier,
the ANTILION. With relays of these a rider can start from Calais or
Brussels, lunch at Paris, dine at Lyons and sup at Marseilles. . . . The
new creations, which can begin in less than five years' time, will give
us. . .
Antiwhales to pull becalmed vessels;
Antisharks to help catch fish;
Antihippopotamuses to pull our river-boats;
Anticrocodiles to help them;
Antiseals or sea-steeds.
All of these brilliant products will be the necessary result of a creation
effected by counter-molded aromas ["arômes contre-moulés"], beginning
with an aromal bath that will purge the seas of their bitumen. (ibid., pp.
254-55)

All of this will occur thanks to Man (i.e., thanks to Fourier, to whom man will have listened):

[Man] is a creature who weighs heavily in the balance of universal destinies; we will see that a scientific error on the part of our globe, a delay in acting, can compromise the entire universe. . . . The sun, although very active in its light-giving function, is hampered in its aromal outpourings by our globe, which can only furnish false aromas as long as it is not in a state of Harmony. [Fourier goes on to describe numerous other malfunctions in the universe resulting from our own dilatoriness. When this ceases:] our globe, with its regenerated aroma, will regain its luminous halo or boreal corona . . . immediately our five satellites will leave their orbits, set off and unite around us. . . . Whereupon the arctic and antarctic icecaps will melt simultaneously . . . we will be provided with . . . precious minerals, enter into telegraphic correspondence. Mercury, our most precious satellite, will teach us to READ. He will transmit to us the alphabet, the declensions, in short the entire grammar of the *unitary harmonic language*, spoken on the sun and on the harmonized planets, and on all the suns and in all the vortices of heaven's canopy. (ibid., pp. 257-61)

Even greater splendors are described at the end of the *Nouveau Monde amoureux*, where the new disposition of the universe is seen in musical terms:

After the concentration [of our universe] and its arrangement in a new pattern . . . the inhabitants of our globe will notice a striking difference between our [planetary] octave and the three octaves which have arrived and become fully active. We shall see that each of them combines five notes or moons on the miniature pedal and that this pedal carries the double ring which is the attribute of all the pedals of the major keyboard, the difference being that the high pedal carries them when their orbit is based on the equator, while the low pedal carries them in a split orbit around the poles. . . . [Fourier goes on to describe cosmic alterations similar to those given in the previous passage]. Then our celestial decor will begin to be suffused with color, by day and by night. We will have for our adornment by day, four prosolar [planets] of various shades, visible in broad daylight. According to their position, other stars like Jupiter and Vesta will retain some of their brightness in the blaze of day. Their alternating appearance will enlighten the nudity of our empyrean which, during the hours of day, is comparable to a large room whose only decor is four bare walls and a big colored lamp in the middle. (VII, 494-95).

III   *Filling the Void*

To explain — or explain away — Fourier's cosmological fantasies either by reference to other authors or to the advances of modern science is — we have suggested — not particularly rewarding. His alteration of the planets' orbits may indeed be no more ridiculous than Hegel's dialectical explanation of the vegetable and animal domains;[12] some of his prophecies have come true or are likely to: Raymond Queneau notes that in 1959 a Soviet engineer proposed to change the earth's climate and create perpetual daylight by forming a ring of microscopic particles around the planet.[13] But these are isolated examples; given the number of Fourier's predictions, it would be surprising if one or two were not realized. Fourier's cosmology should be treated above all as the supreme example of an imagination that, in its apparently wildest flights, is — paradoxically — nonetheless *controlled*. Its audacity is surprising, but the continual references to other aspects of his "system": the contact of extremes, or the laws of analogy and unity, indicate a fruitful collaboration (or tension?) between stasis and movement, the tendency toward order and the tendency toward chaos. This may not exempt Fourier from the charge of madness, but it does suggest that his fantasies may be poetically worthwhile.

If we wish at all costs to relate his cosmology to the world we know, then we might profitably reconsider it in the light of its nontechnological nature. While it may frequently appear magic, it is informed by a deep respect for nature — and human nature — that enable it to be placed, without too much intellectual sleight-of-hand, in the context of modern ecological and biological thought. Industry "destroys forests, dries up springs, stirs up hurricanes and all kinds of atmospheric excesses" (VI, 391). Fourier's remedy is to limit industrial production, reorganize agriculture, and implement a program of reafforestation (Xa, 203), with a view to improving micro-climates and, eventually, the world's climate. And if the seas have not yet turned into lemonade, who would have thought, even twenty years ago, that the Rhine would today be one vast sewer? The change is no more radical than that proposed by Fourier. In Harmony, Man as well as nature, will be "corrected": he will live longer, reproduce less, grow a tail, and become white. In stressing humanity's physical or biological development, and the influence Man can have on his environment, Fourier goes beyond the traditional variety of science fiction, which is concerned above all with the impact of technological sophistication, and shows himself as a precursor of a more modern — perhaps more realisable — kind.

Fourier's cosmogony has one final peculiarity, which seems to deny our last assertion. For in place of the expanding universe which we have now generally come to accept as the "real" one, his ideal one is in a process of *contraction*, for all the talk of "biniverses," "triniverses," and the like. "The eternal silence of these infinite spaces terrifies me," wrote Pascal.[14] Fourier has three answers to Pascal's terror: he populates space by the souls of the dead, thus filling or "furnishing" it;[15] its celestial bodies can communicate with one another and eventually with us; and he proposes to reorganize the universe in order to correct the chaotic expansion it has hitherto undergone. For "condensation . . . is the rule of perfection," he wrote, citing the diamond as proof. "It is the same with universes. Their perfection is directly proportional to their degree of condensation, and nothing demonstrates more clearly the extreme youth and unsophisticated nature of our universe than the enormous spacing that is everywhere apparent" (VII, 485-86). This will naturally be corrected in Harmony:

. . . after the general organization and condensation [which will take place in Harmony] there will be no more than fifty million leagues between the sun and Herschel [Uranus] and fifty thousand million from the sun to the heavenly vault, which will still be linked to the centre ["foyer"] by sidereal chains of varying degrees.

In the place of this unification and concentration, what a sight is our universe, with suns heaped up at random like piles of apples in granaries and empty spaces without proportion or unity. (ibid., 486-87)

However, Fourier's views on contraction should be qualified in two important ways. In the first place, the "contracting" universe still remains enormous; Fourier blandly states that the distance between the center and the spheroid will decrease from 1,300,000,000 leagues to the hardly insignificant 100,000,000 leagues (ibid., p. 486). In the days when the size of the universe was a matter of considerable speculation, such a figure was still immense. It is not impossible that Fourier inflated the "original" size deliberately in order to impress his readers with the still enormous "corrected" size, with the bland presentation turning an overstatement into an apparent understatement. In so doing, he would also be self-consistent, since the dominant characteristic of the calculations concerned with life in Harmony is their immensity.[16] Second, the movement of the celestial bodies is controlled, not arrested: Fourier's universe is a place of intense activity, in keeping with his "ongoing cosmogony." In his ordering of the immensity and depiction of communication between its parts, the Prime Mover, Charles Fourier, creates a cosmic Utopia in which the tendencies toward concentration on the one hand, and proliferation or expansion on the other, are in an extremely delicate equilibrium.

CHAPTER 7

An Æsthetic of Transgression

I *"I Am Only an Inventor . . ."*

WRITERS, like all other inhabitants of Harmony, were promised endless benefits by Fourier (III, 352-60.). In Civilization, most of them have been unhappy, lacking either the initial capital or the "mercantile" sense to live in ease and dignity; the majority have been both poor and the butt of mockery — like inventors (III, 405-08). For Fourier never ceased proclaiming that, although his fate was similar to theirs, he was not a writer or an orator, but an "inventor." Indeed, had he had the talent of an orator, he wrote, he would be, like them, "sterile in genius" (XIb, 232-33). It is clear from his many statements on the subject that he equated style with rhetoric, a kind of useless embellishment of what really mattered. In other words, he made a rigid distinction between what the French call "fond" (content) and "forme" (form), with his preference inevitably going to the former: "I furnish the subject. Let someone else add his prose. People want flowers of rhetoric and clouds of butterfly wings. . . . However devoid of banal ornamentation it may be, isn't the beauty of the subject enough to exempt the author from payment of his tribute of eloquence? We must constantly remember that I am an inventor and not an orator" (VII, 112). Style is opposed to invention, and can be equated with falsity: "Plato and Voltaire were rich in style, but invented nothing . . . posterity will admire my three laws of equitable distribution [capital, work, talent] . . . and shame my detractors who will only have shone by their style" (IX, 610-11). Imagination is the prerogative of novelists, but to praise an inventor for his imagination is to depreciate his scientific methodology (Xa, 127-28).

The irony of this is apparent in retrospect, since posterity has reversed Fourier's main proposition and now values him above all for what might loosely be called his "formal" qualities. For the word "inventor" can be taken in various ways, in English as in French. The inventor is either a discoverer, in the sense that he uncovers something preexisting (the laws of Attraction); or he creates something new or original (Fourier's educational system); or he "imagines in a completely arbitrary fashion, without respecting truth or reality" (*Dictionnaire Robert*: Fourier's cosmogony). In Fourier these are inextricably mixed, the mixture itself — which is both the substance and the manner of the written presentation — providing a puzzle for the general reader. In other words, Fourier the triple inventor doubly destroys our reading expectations: we frequently do not find what his titles promise, and when we do, its presentation is so bizarre that it tests our patience to its limits. For the literary historian, however, this imbroglio provides a means of situating Fourier in the current of creative writing. Whereas "obeying the rules" used to be one of the tokens of æsthetic merit, for the last fifty years or more, the systematic practice of transgression has been seen — rightly or wrongly — as an indication of artistic value.

A steadily growing group of writers (Lautréamont, Nerval, Rimbaud, Roussel, J-P. Brisset, Artaud, Bataille, Butor, Robbe-Grillet and others) can be studied for the same reason as Fourier. They are all characterized by their radical departure from the norms of literary usage, a departure which may be due to naivety, as in the case of Brisset, or sophisticated calculation with Roussel. The departure brings into question many of the most basic notions and preconceptions we possess: among them genre, "literarity" (the features that enable a text to be called literary), and the operations of language itself. Fourier's naive imaginative gifts and his autodidact's self-confident ignorance mark his writings in such a way that he is a precursor of those who have, by their own literary practice, liberated *our* imagination and sharpened our awareness of how language functions. In our first chapter we examined what is perhaps the major impediment to reading Fourier: his constant juxtaposition of different kinds of discourse. In the pages that follow, we shall attempt to describe and explain certain other widespread transgressive phenomena in his writings.

II   *Transgression of the Unit*

By unit, we mean various linguistic and mathematical signs: the word, the letters of the alphabet, punctuation marks, and numbers. All of these are altered or "corrected" in various ways by Fourier, whose ability to meddle with *everything*, from the humble comma to the planet Venus, is quite astonishing.

Among Fourier's most widespread linguistic activities is the creation of neologisms. They are justified by him on the most reasonable, indeed the only grounds: that a new meaning needs a new word (V, 311, note); his "defence and illustration" of the procedure in the *Théorie de l'unité universelle* (II, 99-102, second pagination) also adopts the by now familiar ploy of ridiculing others such as Leibniz (for "monads"), Kant (for "noumenon"), or even Aristotle (for "quiddities" and "entitatules"). Among the words Fourier invents — and justifies — in this section are: "Prae," "Post," "Citra," "Ultra," "Cis," "Trans," "Avant" (fore-), and "Arrière" (after-, as in "Arrière-propos" or Afterword), "Intro" and "Extro" (as in "Extroduction"), all of which are "distributive" prefixes used (a) in the description of series and (b) in the disposition of his own works. The reason for the second use has already been noted: by analogy with the fundamental laws governing the arrangement of series, the *description* of the serial system must be similarly ordered.[1] The second class described in the same piece includes "technical" words: "passional," "attractional," "Seriism," "Guaranteeism," "Harmonian," "Solitone," etc. For instance, individuals are "passionate," whereas "passional" qualifies the "general mechanism": hence "the passional world" or "the attractional mechanism." Fourier does not explain "solitone," "bitone," etc. on this occasion. These adjectives are in fact used to designate the number of passions present in each individual (i.e., a "solitone" has only one passion, a "bitone" two, and so on), and show clearly the importance of musical terminology in his work.

A large class of neologisms is formed by words qualifying relationships of love or friendship, beginning with "céladonie," which is the name Fourier gives to spiritual love. The vocabulary is formed by putting two Greek words together: "mono" (etc.) + "philos," giving "monophilie," "hémiphilie," "androphilie," and so on. Thus the varying ways in which bonds of friendship are formed are described. For instance, "monophilie" is the relationship between any two individuals, where only one of the aspects of friendship is involved. Similarly, "mono" + "gamos" (marriage) gives "monogamie," "androgamie," "phanérogamie," and so on. "Ultragamie" is thus (?) the name for a female homosexual relationship, since it is harmony to the seventh degree, which always involves the kind of "spilling over" of the love relationship between two sexes which becomes "enmeshed" with "the passion of friendship or uni-sexual affection" (IV, 367). In case this is not enough, Fourier on occasion refines these gradations to take account of the difference between the sexes, using the roots "andrie" and "gynie" respectively to denote relationships between men and women: the relationship between Theseus and Pirithoüs or Orestes and Pylades becomes "androphilie," or the friendship of two men.[2]

The real originality of many neologisms, it has been pointed out by Michel Butor, lies in the creation of masculine nouns from feminine ones: another, linguistic, manifestation of Fourier's program for female emancipation.[3] The reverse is the grammatical norm for, as Butor also notes, "the masculine has priority" in French: for example, where a pronoun stands for a million women and one man, it is still considered masculine for the purposes of agreement. The reason for feminine priority invoked by Fourier is a splendid example of his consistency and some compensation for the difficulties he is in over assigning Love, together with Familyism, to the "minor" mode:[4] "I place the female fairies ["fées"] before the male ones ["fés"] because in all relationships in the minor mode, women have precedence over men" (IV, 373). Thus, alongside "fés", we have "vestels" (< "vestales"), "matrons" (< "matrones"), "sibyls" (< "sybilles"), and the very odd "bonnin" (< "bonne": maid), to give just a few examples. The reverse also occurs: "cherubine" (< "chérubin": cherub), "séraphine" (< "séraphin": seraph): doubtless by analogy with the regular "bambin, -ine" (urchin, tot). There also exists the extremely curious "royesse" and "reinin" (VIII, 219), which mean, respectively, the wife of a king and the husband of a queen. These terms are necessary in Harmony since there are equal numbers of male and female thrones and most royal couples will not be married. Fourier is anxious to make quite clear that the husband of a queen is not necessarily or even usually a king. Her status is, in this instance, superior to his, and a term must be invented, on the basis of an existing word, to account for the difference.

What is ultimately at stake is the whole concept of gender. In creating masculine nouns from feminine ones Fourier is explicitly defending female rights, while the creation of words such as "séraphine" or "royesse" is essentially an act of clarification and a means of ensuring *grammatical* equity. The final step is to change and even invent gender in keeping with the role of the noun concerned. Fourier's "Plan of the Treatise of Passionate Attraction" sets out its parts in two octaves, each of which has a major and a minor "keyboard" ("clavier"). As major is the "dominant masculine mode," the sun, which is analogous with the "pivotal major section," is given its normal gender, masculine ("le"); in the minor (feminine) mode, the sun becomes feminine ("la"), being analogous with the "minor pivotal section" of that part; it becomes neuter ("lo") when it is analogous with the "pivotal mixed section." This is an isolated, even unique example in Fourier's writings. Its importance is nonetheless considerable as a token of his attitude toward language, which is exactly the same as his attitude toward the social organization of his time or the cosmos: if it is not consonant with the (arbitrary) system he invents, then it must be changed. In other words, there is no possibility for "give and take," since it never occurred to Fourier that he — and not the rest of the universe — might be out of step. Fourier's use of analogy or metaphor transgresses normal metaphorical practice (which is partly dependent on cultural acceptance) for the same reason.

Fourier's transgression of the alphabet is quite consistent. He accepts spelling conventions (except when he invents words) and uses the usual signs, but inverts them, reverses them, or places them on their side when he wishes to indicate certain serial functions. Thus ✕ and X are respectively: pivot and counterpivot (or counterpivotal group) of a series; Y and Λ are direct and inverse pivots; K and ꓘ indicate "ambiguous" or transitional groups, in ascending or descending order (VI,v). The signs are important, as they indicate contrast or harmony ("accord": harmony or chord) within a series, and are in theory an aid to "decoding" it. We will leave readers to decide for themselves the clarity of Fourier's specimen series:

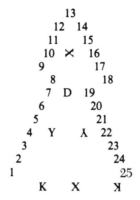

✕ — pivotal group		Y — ascending group subpivot	
X — counter-pivotal group		⅄ — descending group subpivot	
K — ambiguous [transitional ascending group]		D — diffracting group [in half-harmony with all the others]	

(VI, 63-64)

According to Simone Debout, some of the signs used are really distortions of certain letters of the Greek alphabet: ℩ (gamma), ⅄ (lambda), ⅄ (khi), while the mathematical sign ∞ becomes ✕ to denote the pivot.[5] Whether or not this is the case, the process involved in taking a letter of the alphabet to stand as a sign for something else, without even the motivation of its being an initial letter of its *significatum* (e.g., "A" for "ambiguous") is very strange. Only when we know the third term and can accept the substitution (e.g., that ✕ may stand for ∞ can the sign become motivated for us. Until that time, it has to be accepted as arbitrary and needs explanation by the author. Exactly the same problem is posed by Fourier's analogies.

Fourier ultimately tired of the Western alphabet in its present form and proposed various reforms, including "unitary typography" (VI, 480, n.1). Disappointingly, only the framework is given, with no real indication of the new signs to be used (forty-eight in all), although it appears that the present letters would form the basis, but be disposed differently (e.g. ᴚ would denote "thick" (?) "r"). In the same footnote, Fourier foreshadows a new system of punctuation (which he claims he had already invented but lost . . .) with twenty-five signs, including four different kinds of comma, a new system of musical notation based on twelve lines,[6] and a method of counting based on twelve instead of ten. . . .[7]

The final example of what we have called the transgression of the unit is again isolated, but one which brings into doubt the whole of our — and Fourier's — system of meanings. The units are the word and the phoneme, and the procedure is the play on words known as homophony. Fourier only indulged in it once in a manuscript that was first published some fourteen years ago and has recently been the object of a critical edition by Simone Debout.[8] For obvious reasons, the procedure is untranslatable. The first sentence runs thus: "Geai ressue mât chair l'or, lin vite à sion queue tu mats à dresser pourras l'air dix nez rats sein ment dés, dix manches d'œufs sept ambre," which can be reconstituted in normal French: "J'ai reçu, ma chère Laure, l'invitation que tu m'as adressée pour aller dîner à Saint-Mandé, dimanche deux septembre" — or a banal reply to a dinner invitation. Readers familiar with French will note that the actual disruption of the word, in terms of spelling, is relatively unimportant: virtually all the words in the sentence (homophonous version) can be found in a reasonably sized dictionary. Nor does the punctuation have to be altered to obtain a "normal" version of the manuscript. On the other hand, the homophony is not always word for word (as in "reçue," which gives "ressue"), for the phonemes are frequently redistributed (e.g., "l'invitation" gives "l'in vite à sion"). What then is the "sense" of this strange manuscript?

Simone Debout undertakes a Freudian reading, while giving reasons for the linguistic importance of the piece: "Fourier does not destroy what constitutes language, the enigmatic meeting of sounds and sense. He does not break with language. He shows that cultural and social habits reduce its possibilities" (p. 104). Whereas his analogies between cauliflowers and love, or the giraffe and truth, are "nonsense," the sexual imagery created by the associations within the homophonous manuscript is "almost universal" (p. 43). The first statement is, we believe, eminently reasonable, although the second seriously underestimates the significance of Fourier's analogical "system."

Indeed, we are inclined to reverse Mme Debout's statements. For what is involved here is in a way far more arbitrary than Fourier's analogies, since, in the case of homophony, it is linguistic

arbitrariness (the relationship between "signifier" and "signified") which allows it to occur. To give one example in English,
the phrase "the sun's rays meet" can be restructured lexically to
give "the sons raise meat" because, phonically, it is identical with
the new version. Very often, the exercise is treated as a game. Its
importance is, however, twofold: it underlines one of the fundamentals of language (the arbitrary relationship between "signifier"
and "signified"), and in so doing it generates semantic divergen-
ces on the basis of phonic identity. It is therefore clearly related to
rhyme, with one crucial difference. For rhyme, as has been demonstrated, can combine phonic and semantic equivalence (synonymy
or antonymy). When Emily Dickinson writes:

> Time is a test of trouble,
> But not a remedy.
> If such it prove, it prove too
> There was no malady.[9]

the combination of the phonic and the semantic in the antony-
mous rhymes makes a powerful contribution toward the unity of
the stanza from which they are taken.

The interest of homophony is precisely that it tends to destroy
any sense-creating operation: juxtaposition of the original text
and the homophonous version will inevitably produce incongruity
rather than motivated difference, and may well devalue the former.
Or, to return to and develop Mme Debout's first point, whereas
poetry tends to reinforce our belief that sound and sense are
somehow related, the practice of homophony destroys this particular cultural expectation. It is a disturbing process, as the very
existence of Mme Debout's own remarkable attempt at recuperation testifies. It is also, we believe, the counterpart of or complement to Fourier's analogies. Even if the initial step is arbitrary
(why, to take one of his best-known examples [VI, 461], is yellow
and not red or green analogous with paternity?), it is not seen as
such by Fourier, whose belief in the unity of (his) universe and the
role of analogy in creating that unity is unshakable. But the homophonous experiment is not susceptible to the kind of control he
wished to exercise over his analogies. The fact that he did not
apparently repeat the experience may remind us of Ferdinand de
Saussure's abandonment of his researches into anagrams in Greek

and Latin poets. Because he was not completely convinced that what he had uncovered was the result of a tradition, rather than an arbitrary construction of his own based on a random distribution of phonemes in the text, he eventually gave up.[10] It may well be that, frightened by what he had turned up — particularly if Mme Debout's interpretation is correct — Fourier decided to experiment no more, and returned to the analogical universe he had created.

III   *Transgression through Analogy*

We have already discussed in some detail the theoretical and practical role of analogy in Fourier: as an illustration of the "contact of extremes," a manifestation of Man's power in the cosmos, a corollary of the four movements, and above all as a means of ordering chaos.[11] As Fourier's analogies have been seen as anticipating the metaphorical practice of the Surrealists,[12] their *modus operandi* must now be examined.

Metaphor, as normally understood, is a form of compressed simile, or the "use of a word or phrase literally denoting one kind of object or idea in place of another by way of suggesting a likeness or analogy between them" (Webster). When we say "that man is a lion" or refer to "the winter of life," we are relying on the fact that, in the first case, the man and the lion have a common attribute, courage. In the second case, various connotations of winter: cold, the end of the year rather than the beginning of a new one, and so on, enable us to understand that old age is implied. This is of course a gross oversimplification, which omits two crucial factors. First, the role of context: for the man to be seen as a lion, he must have been depicted performing a courageous task. The metaphor would be absurd — or ironical — if he had just run away from someone. Second, the weighting of attributes: if the ones not common to both parts of the metaphor are numerous and/or important, then it is likely to be seen as "weak," and rejected, or just not understood.[13] But these elementary observations can serve as a starting-point for an examination of one or two of Fourier's analogies.

The first involves the humble cauliflower in an unusual role — as an "emblem" of love without obstacles or mystery:

The cauliflower is the counterpart of *the cabbage*, depicting the opposite situation, *love without obstacle or mystery*, the frolicking of *youth* as it flits from pleasure to pleasure. Thus the *cauliflower* is an ocean of *flowers*, an image of the charms of *youth*. . . . (VI, 462, our italics)

The problem is obviously: what common element do the two terms possess? If we use the minimal unit of meaning or "seme," breaking down each word or lexeme into its semic components, we can see which one(s) intersect or overlap, as in the case of the man or the lion: MAN (human + masculine + courageous [contextual seme]) = LION (animal + masculine + courageous). In this example, the man is the "compared," and the lion the "comparer."[14] But in the case of the cauliflower and love without obstacles or mystery, there appears to be no common unit of meaning: CAULIFLOWER (vegetable + visible flowers + leaves [etc.]) vs. YOUTH (human + masculine or feminine + young [etc.]). In this case, both the cauliflower and youth can be considered as comparer and compared. In fact, the emblem can only function, we believe, as a result of an opposition, plus a doubtful correlate of the object opposed to the cauliflower (the cabbage), followed by a chain of very shaky "equivalences" or oppositions:

Cabbage (flowers hard to find) = mystery of love
                vs.
Cauliflower (easy to find flowers) = love without mystery → youth → charm → visible flowers → cauliflower

Most of Fourier's analogies (tautologies?) are based on these third (or fourth or fifth) terms, similarly dubious homologies, or false syllogisms. The other difficulty — but a potentially useful one — which is highlighted by the example is just what constitutes comparer or compared: precisely what is the cauliflower being compared with? If we may indulge in one of Fourier's "metaphors," love is qualified by such an avalanche of attributes that it risks, like the flowers of the cabbage, being buried beneath them. A longer example will demonstrate the complexity and confused nature of the processes involved:

. . . the goldfinch, whose head is covered in red, thus [bathes] in the color of ambition, according to the preceding scale. This bird is the opposite of the canary: its mud-gray but clean and glossy plumage indicates industrious poverty. It represents the child, born of poor parents, who is well-disciplined and brought up to be ambitious and determined to get on. It [the goldfinch] is preoccupied with this idea, and by analogy, its brain is steeped in red, the color of ambition. Its warbling, the emblem of a cultivated mind, is equal to that of the canary, which portrays the rich child with good teachers. Thus the poor but motivated child will attain the same level of education as the child whose family is well-off. . . . As he will achieve this through the help of his family alone, nature has colored his [whose?] wing-feathers yellow to show that his progress is due to their support, to the group of paternity represented by yellow. This poor child will not be frightened by the thorny problems ["ronces" = brambles] of science. He will overcome the difficulties of learning. . . . By analogy, the goldfinch likes thistles, spiky plants having an affinity with the peasant class who are used to the trials ["epines" = thorns] of hard work. In order to show these relationships, nature has given two contrasting creatures a common bond of sympathy with the thistle ["chardon"]: the goldfinch ["chardonneret"], emblem of the studious child of peasant stock, and the donkey, emblem of the peasant, his *patois* or ridiculous braying, his resignation to harsh treatment, and his stupid persistence in using faulty methods. . . . Without analogy, nature is but a mass of thorns. . . . (VI, 461)

It is virtually impossible to render diagrammatically the mind-boggling equivalences in this long passage, since it contains at least four major interrelated analogical propositions, and indulges simultaneously in wordplay, using metaphors to explain the analogies. The major propositions or syllogisms are (we think) basically as follows:

(I)   (a)   Red is the color of ambition.
      (b)   The goldfinch is predominantly red.
      (c)   The goldfinch is the emblem of the (poor) ambitious child.

In logic, the third part of the statement is incorrect, since the only conclusion one can draw is that the goldfinch is predominantly the color of ambition. In strict logic, two more steps are necessary. If we were to reconstitute Fourier's thought processes — or, to be more accurate, reconstitute the tortuous logical itinerary his mind has clearly not followed — we could say that he moves from statements (a) and (b) above to (c) by assuming that an object (goldfinch) which has a color (red) symbolizing a certain property (ambition) can serve as the emblem of another object (poor ambitious child) which has the property in question.[15]

(II) (a)   Yellow is the color of paternity or familyism.
      (b)   The goldfinch/poor child has yellow in his wings.
      (c)   The poor child is helped by his family.

Here the most extraordinary part of the statement is the second. In the original French it passes almost unnoticed, since Fourier uses the possessive pronoun "son" (his) to refer back to the child *or* the goldfinch. The grammatical antecedent is the child, but it has to be confused with the goldfinch in order to help make this particular section of the extended analogy work.

(III) (a)   The child is like the goldfinch.
      (b)   The child is not afraid of the thorns of science.
      (c)   The goldfinch likes thistles.

The main difficulty here is that, in order to get the syllogism to begin to work, one has to accept the figurative part of the second term and to replace (b) by something like "the child likes thistles." In other words, the analogy depends on a metaphor.

(IV) (a)   The goldfinch is the emblem of the (poor, ambitious) peasant child.
      (b)   The goldfinch likes thistles.
      (c)   The donkey likes thistles.

This is perhaps the most glaring example of compressed logic. In order to begin to understand the proposition one has first to accept that the most important attribute of the child is now his peasant origins; and then that the donkey is the emblem of the peasant (father) and is *contrasted* with the goldfinch. . . . Of course Fourier explains all this, but in such a way that it is irreducible to any logic without a whole chain of syllogisms.

Various conclusions can now be drawn about Fourier's analogical practice. The first is that the starting-point is rapidly left behind by a whole series of propositions or ramifications — with or without the help of "compressed" logic. The basic reason is inherent in the system itself: everything is analogous to everything else, but the analogies are made to function by a series of exterior terms or propositions (both our examples), themselves sometimes dependent on other propositions. The second is that the initial proposition is arbitrary (red = ambition), and the rest in theory motivated: Fourier's analogies might therefore appear, at first sight, to cut across the distinction between the (nonmotivated) linguistic sign and the (motivated) symbol. In fact, the motivation of what follows the initial comparison is apparent rather than real, as the very shaky logic of the succeeding propositions demonstrates. For *other* analogies can equally well be deduced from them, which might suit Fourier very well, but which testifies to the shakiness of his reasoning — and to the "openness" of the system. We have come a very long way from the "fixed" science he extolled.

That the analogies need a third or fourth term to make them work is not unusual, however. Umberto Eco, in an article on the semantics of metaphor, based largely on a reading of *Finnegan's Wake*, notes for instance that the relationship in the book between Minucius and Mandrake is motivated by the existence of a third term, Felix. The reader, he notes, relies very heavily on "a very long series of third terms which exist in the general context of the book."[16] Eco goes on to propose a model for metaphor, as follows:

$$A \quad vs \quad B \quad vs \quad C \quad vs \quad D$$
$$\downarrow \qquad \downarrow \qquad \downarrow \qquad \downarrow$$
$$X \qquad Y \qquad Z \qquad K$$

The horizontal axis is semantic or antonymic, and the vertical one designates cultural connotations. Thus, when A is replaced by B, the metaphor is banal, an antonymic substitution. If it is replaced by X, the substitution is again simple, but occurs as a result of cultural connotations. If A is replaced by K, the operation forms a "daring" or transgressive metaphor. In other words, the intermediate steps are jumped, rather like Fourier's analogies.

From this it might indeed appear that Fourier's basic premiss — everything is connected to everything else — is validated. On the contrary, Eco affirms that "in practice, there are millions of empty valences and millions of units which cannot be connected" (p. 40). Why? Because of the importance of the cultural or social factor. As Eco again writes: "Imagination would not have the capacity to invent (or to recognize) a metaphor unless culture

provided — in the form of a possible structure of a global semantic system — the underlying network of arbitrarily determined
contiguities" (p. 36). Whether a metaphor is accepted or understood or not depends ultimately on the social context and a
consensus of what "reality" is, even though reality is subsequently
forgotten (pp. 37-38, 43). Thus, even if it may be possible to
provide, *after Fourier's own explanation*, the "correct" links
between A (red) and K (the poor ambitious child), the comparison
is still unlikely to be acceptable. What each reader must decide for
himself is whether Fourier's analogies are of the "daring" or
inventive sort, which are a powerful means of extending our
sensibility, or whether they do nothing for us at all. The demands
of culture and logic are insistent, even if they are not recognized
as such.

Does this then render Fourier's analogies "nonpoetic"? The
network of comparisons involving the goldfinch, the poor
ambitious child, the thistle, and the donkey may indeed be illogi-
cal, even tedious. But the idea that red is the color of ambition is
sufficiently striking for us to imagine our own, culturally acceptable, analogies based on this equivalence. After all, Fourier
imagines the inhabitants of Harmony playing "hunt (or invent)
the analogy." Why should not his readers? In other words, we
would make a distinction between the more or less arbitrary
"primary" — unexplained and unexplainable — analogies, and
the network of secondary — explainable, close to metaphor, and
tedious — analogies that support them. Many of Fourier's most
imaginative passages are based on *implicit* analogies, although
within them others may be made explicit. *Because* man copulates,
therefore the stars copulate (the universe is animistic). Androgynes
are part of the heritage of classical mythology (and in turn, like all
myths, respond to a fundamental human need or aspiration),
therefore the notion of an androgynous planet is culturally
acceptable, once we accept the primary analogy — which we
should do, since animism is a very powerful notion.

In this way, Fourier does indeed create a universe of correspondences (almost in spite of himself, we are tempted to say). In so
doing, in a sense he "democratizes" metaphor. One of Jean
Ricardou's complaints about traditional metaphorical usage is
that the "comparer" is subordinated to the "compared":[17] the
lion is "used" by the man, "courage" is extracted from the com-

parison, and then the animal is discarded. This never happens in Fourier, for two reasons. First, the dissimilarity of comparer and compared is so great that it is a guarantee of the continuing equal status of both terms. But secondly, that status is dependent on other comparisons, in an analogical or homological network. Nothing stands on its own, semantically speaking, but takes on meaning according to its context. Fourier's analogies thus obey one of the fundamental rules of language, although many of them may disobey logic and the demands of even "daring" metaphorical usage.

In the final analysis, however, Fourier's practice of analogy undermines the very system it is supposed to justify. The danger with "all is related to all," as Michel Foucault has shown, is that it leads to a system turning endlessly upon itself, or universal sameness.[18] But as we have seen, the analogies "get away from" Fourier. The detail proliferates, analogy producing and being produced by analogy in a process that transcends Fourier's control. In a passage about analogies published after his death, Fourier comes close to admitting the "play" in his system:

Readers should beware of these generalized [analogical] instructions. *The theory of movement and analogy is subject to a whole host of complications which would belie the general calculations.* For example, Mercury, although it is a satellite of the earth and a star of the major octave, the most precious of the keyboard of friendship, nevertheless operates in the keyboard of love, creating a kernelled fruit, the most beautiful of all: the peach. Why then is a star of the major octave engaged in the minor one? Don't rush to ask these questions. I will treat them in good time. . . . (XII, 121, our italics)

In short, the system *almost* works. In its general outline it is indeed arbitrary and tautologous, "proving" itself by itself, just as the analogies in theory support one another in a network of causality. But in practice, many strain logic to its limits, being replaceable by almost any others we care to invent by using the same terms, and are culturally unacceptable. There are, we have suggested, two poles, or series of poles, in Fourier: on the one hand, the tendency toward centrality, concentration, stasis; on the other, a system of relationships without one central point, having a tendency toward proliferation. Fourier's writings on the cosmos appear to embody both tendencies; the descriptions of life in

Harmony are such that the overwhelming tendency of Utopia toward concentration is negated, in particular by the notion of the "place." Traditional analogical systems frequently have God the ultimate reference point or center. At the center of Fourier's is, of course, himself. But he is a God who is not quite in control of the detail, and who on one occasion at least seems aware of this.

IV *Tables*

Roland Barthes notes that one of the delights of Fourier is the way in which context and hierarchy are constantly ignored by his illustrations.[19] His remark can be generalized to cover all aspects of Fourier's writings. The major problem posed by the organization of each book, we have suggested, is that of deciding which level of discourse is the one against which the others may be evaluated. This raises in turn the interrelated problems of humor and irony. The juxtaposition of the disparate is the main characteristic of each work taken as a whole and, within it, of many chapters or sections. When we examine the detail of what is said, the same applies, with the disparate and the incongruent being brought together in a manner that clearly prefigures the Surrealists. If "the encounter, on an operating table, of a sewing machine and an umbrella" (Lautréamont quoted by André Breton) is the essence of Surrealist imagery, then Fourier's concatenation of goldfinches, thistles, donkeys, peasants, and ambition clearly warrants this label. The difference between Fourier and the Surrealists, as Breton has indicated, is that Fourier's (primary?) analogies are "prefabricated" rather than spontaneous[20] (even if the logic of the prefabrication is suspect). The "secondary" analogies are also explained in often ponderous terms, whereas the effectiveness of the Surrealist metaphor lies in its quality of immediacy and surprise. This is why Fourier's initial or "primary" analogies are closer to Surrealist practice and ultimately more poetic than the secondary ones, whose value as subversive elements within his own system is nonetheless considerable. Parodying Breton, we are inclined to say that, in Fourier, the encounter *within a table*, of jonquils and maternal love, or tulips and individual justice, is what renders his work poetic in a Surrealist sense:

Hieroglyphs in the vegetable domain

K	THE GERANIUM	*Serial Industry*	

Odoriferous	*Polianthes,*	The emancipated woman about town.
	Hyacinth,	The restrained woman about town.
	Jonquil,	Maternal love.
	Heliotrope,	A sordid mind.
Inodorous	*China-aster,*	The good housewife.
	Buttercup	Court etiquette.
	Anemone,	Well-to-do upstarts.
	Tulip,	Individual Justice.
Infantile	*Jasmine,*	Childish Ambition
	Pansy	Choruses under the age of puberty.
	Violet,	Hardworking infants.
	Bear's ear,	Studious children.
	MALLOW,	*Civilized ambition* (IV, 239)

The normal function of a table is to explain something, to save space. Fourier's tables, we suggested in our opening chapter, need to be explained, the relationship between table and text thereby being reversed and space being "wasted." We would only modify our statement in one way. If we emphasize the discursive aspect of Fourier's writing, taking it in the way in which he intended it, as a treatise passing from premises to conclusions, then the tables are in urgent need of explanation. If we ignore the discursive aspect — which Fourier invites us to do because it is brought into question by the heterogeneity of his discourse — then the tables can become the basis of our own analogical play, which will complement the "play" within his system.

CHAPTER 8

Fourier and Utopia

I Characteristics of Utopia

"WHAT is Utopia? It is the dream of well-being without the means of execution, without an effective method. Thus all philosophical sciences are Utopias, for they have always led peoples to the very opposite of the state of well-being they promised them" (XIb, 356). This hostile definition of Utopia is a token of Fourier's general intolerance of anything that might bear some comparison with his own ideas. Robert Owen, the Saint-Simonians, the author of *Télémaque*, and indeed anyone who believed in human perfectibility or who had dared to imagine a better society, were treated with the scorn born of his suspicious self-defensiveness.[1] The irony is of course that Fourier is labeled a Utopian writer by all histories of literature and dictionaries of biography. While the label is, we believe, justified in a general sense, his writings oblige us to reexamine the fairly large group of characteristics that have come to be accepted as typical of that happy place called Utopia. We are not claiming that Utopia should be redefined, although more precision in definition is needed, but that the term needs very careful qualification if it is to be used in respect of Fourier. Many major aspects of Utopia are either not present in his work or presented in such a way as to change totally their significance. Yet again a subversive process is at work; on this occasion the very genre to which his writings are supposed to belong is under implicit attack.

The word "Utopia," first used by Thomas More in 1516 for the title of his book, is of Greek derivation — *ou-topos* or possibly *eu-topos* — and means therefore "nowhere" or "happy place." In practice, it has come to mean both simultaneously. There is considerable agreement about the basic features of Utopia, although Utopian writing shades off very rapidly into other genres such as the imaginary voyage, science fiction, or Arcadia. Many of the characteristics are not particularly attractive to many people, and there have been various attempts at defining a kind of mentality or psychology common to Utopian writers, a psychology which is in its turn rather negative: "infantile" is one word that has been used to describe the personality which creates an imaginary, Utopian world.[2] The drawback of this kind of approach is its extremely reductive nature, whereby the enormous variety of Utopian writings is assimilated to a few basic mental types.

Among the most common — and unattractive — features of Utopia (we make no distinction between the literary and nonliterary variety) are its regularity and its static nature. Utopia is an ideal society in an ideal setting, and as such it is not susceptible to change. As all is perfect, nothing can be improved, and nothing really happens. Time, as the dimension within which events of any kind occur, is abolished precisely by the insistence on the regular temporal division of the day: as Gilles Lapouge explains in a recent monograph, the discovery of abstract time abolishes time as duration, and the mechanical clock is a Utopian invention, "correcting" time and perfecting nature.[3] The inhabitants of this timeless or timeful, regulated and regular society are either reduced to complete uniformity or have their allotted place in a rigid hierarchy, which are really two ways of doing the same thing. In More's *Utopia*, the numbers in each "family" are strictly determined, depending on whether it is a city or country group, and in turn various dignitaries ("Philarchs" and "Archiphilarchs") are appointed on the basis of one for so many families. Communal eating, sleeping, and living are features of many Utopias, although they need not exclude various classes of diners seated at tables according to their status — as in Fourier's Phalansteries.

The regularity and perfection of Utopia indicate a rather special relationship between the Utopian writer and nature. The outside world, in the sense of a milieu in which growth, birth, and death occur, the domain of insects, animals, vegetation, and weather, is generally abhorred on account of its uncontrolled, rampant nature. But "mathematical" nature, or the cosmos, provides an ideal model, one in which change cannot occur, since it has been regulated once and for all by the Deity.[4] Campanella's *City of the Sun*, by its name and disposition, with a temple in the center surrounded by seven concentric circles, is perhaps the most striking example of this feature. In practice, the favorite form of Utopia, topographically speaking, is the city. Its shape may or may not represent Man's idea of the cosmos, but its existence as such marks it as a human creation and is a testimony to Man's power. It is as it were midway between the family unit — generally rejected by Utopian writers — and the State, forming the "minimal representation of the social relationship":[5] the family link is a nonpolitical one, whereas to take humanity as the representation of the social relationship is to lose the notion of community. The finite nature of the city enables it to be *seen* as an image of the cosmos, of the family, and of humanity.[6] Utopian cities are always carefully planned — no rebuilding is ever necessary — with the planning itself yet another aspect of the perfection of Utopia.

The ideal city constitutes a finite, closed space. The space outside is either nonexistent, in that it is not described, or forms a kind of aqueous or terrestrial barrier, a deterrent to potential intruders: Utopia is frequently an island or continent (e.g., More's *Utopia*; Bacon's *New Atlantis*; Mercier's *La Terre Australe*) or a remote, inaccessible land delimited by natural geographical features. In order to reach Eldorado, the travelers in Voltaire's *Candide* encounter both kinds of obstacle: they are carried by a torrent through a tunnel under precipitous mountains. When they leave the realm, a special machine has to be invented to carry them over the cliffs surrounding it. The castle in Sade's *The 120 Days of Sodom* is accessible only — and then with difficulty — to the select few who will engage in the orgies there. Utopia does not normally welcome trade or visitors — except those willing to marvel and subsequently to describe it. Utopians seldom travel beyond the confines of their realm (*Candide*; *Télémaque*) since there is no point in their leaving perfection behind them. Within Utopia they may, in cases where the city somehow merges into a larger but still well-delineated space, although it is not clear what they gain from this, since everywhere they must encounter the same. The ten-yearly house-change lottery in More's *Utopia* may well be a device to break the monotony, rather like the absurd ritual of regular car-changing in contemporary Western society.

It is not difficult to imagine the kind of moral and political structure this kind of city or realm will have. Utopia is highly institutionalized, since there is really very little for the people to do other than govern themselves or be governed. One of the most important institutions is the educational one, for it is essential that all citizens understand and conform to the society into which they are born. Many Utopias place great emphasis on pedagogy and the general rearing of children, who are frequently brought up communally (e.g., Campanella). Sexual mores are very tightly controlled by elaborate systems of laws and taboos, with the control usually taking the form of limiting the amount and kind of activity. On the whole, sex and Utopia do not mix very well. In More's *Utopia* there is strict monogamy, adultery is an offence, and sex before marriage is forbidden; in Fénelon's realm of La Bétique, purity and monogamy are the rule; while in the *New Atlantis* of Bacon, chastity is one of the great virtues. There are exceptions of course, notably that of Rabelais' Abbaye de Thélème, with its motto "Fay ce que vouldras" (Do what you will), but it is arguable that Rabelais is not a Utopian writer at all.[7]

Nevertheless, it is not God or a deity who is normally invoked to protect or sanctify chastity and monogamy, but the institutions of Utopia. Religion or religions may well exist there, but their role is relatively unimportant: there is no point in striving for perfection if everything is perfect, and a deity is little more than yet another guarantee that the system works. As for disease, filth, and death, they naturally have no place in the ideal city, and are normally just ignored by Utopian writers. Significantly, More stresses the importance of the Utopians' health, while in Samuel Butler's *Erewhon*, illness is regarded as a crime. In short, Utopias tend to be both aseptic and ascetic. Cleanliness, abstemiousness, and virtue reign, crime is unknown (although the judicial apparatus may be elaborate), and the inhabitants enjoy themselves — if that is the right word — in a remarkably restrained manner. Clearly, something has to give, as it does in Pierre Boulle's recent "counter-Utopia," *Les Jeux de l'esprit* (1971). After years of living in an environment where everything is taken care of, people find that they are unable to take any decisions at all. In order to put a little spice back into life, the world government invents a series of increasingly elaborate and brutal games, culminating in nuclear war. . . .

The commercial and economic organization of Utopias is characterized by the same spirit of self-abnegation. Commerce is thought to be dishonest, private property is abolished, and money is scorned. The inhabitants of Eldorado ignore the precious stones that litter the ground, and those of Fénelon's La Bétique despise gold and silver. An agricultural economy is quite common, its existence in no way contradicting the particular antinatural bias of Utopias, since the practice of agriculture is a way of domesticating nature. Here again, Utopia merges into another genre, the land of Cockaigne with its emphasis on eating or, as one commentator puts it, "a compensatory dream born of oral frustration."[8] Scientific Utopias are rare until the nineteenth century, with the exception of Francis Bacon's *New Atlantis*, and in any case are arguably science fiction. As for industry, it is again not until the nineteenth century that it appears to play any role in the economic organization of Utopia, thanks to the Saint-Simonians. But whatever the form of economic organization, it is of relatively minor importance alongside other aspects of the ideal community. If, as has been claimed, Utopia is born of a dissatisfaction with the status quo, the written counterpart to active revolt (e.g., More versus his contemporary Machiavelli), then the dissatisfaction appears to be primarily moral and political.[9]

On the whole, the picture we have drawn of Utopia must seem a rather depressing, even sinister one. Sameness, uniformity, monotony, and puritanism are consistent components of the ideal city-state, at least in its traditional form. Utopias are seldom if ever amusing places to visit (at least not intentionally so), even if they are sometimes bizarre. Many are boring, and some are informed by a kind of dry didacticism, others by an implicit bitterness toward the real world to which they are a fictional reply. One of the lessons we may learn from them is how easily would-be humanitarianism can turn into totalitarianism. In an attempt to reconcile the well-being of the individual with that of society, it seems that, in the end, the former is sacrificed: "In the name of human dignity, the new man is made part of the well-oiled, totally dehumanized machine in which he is only a cog."[10]

The fictional presentation of Utopia is also frequently felt by readers to be unsatisfactory, since it is an essentially *descriptive* genre.[11] A favorite device is for someone to tell the future author about his journey to the ideal city or land (More; Campanella; Etienne Cabet, *Voyage en Icarie*); otherwise, the narrator simply relates his own visit (Samuel Butler). An alternative is for the description to appear as a kind of digression or interlude in a story (*Télémaque*; *Candide*). But in all cases the essential construction is:

narration $\longrightarrow$	description	$\longrightarrow$	narration
(framework)	(Utopia)		(framework)

The main characteristic of what might be called the descriptive space of Utopia is repetition, metonymy, "identity which is the movement of difference," whereas narrative fiction is essentially a series of transformations of content.[12] In other words, the Utopian genre only fulfills with difficulty the conditions under which a story may be said to exist, which is why we feel instinctively that it lacks something. "I met a man who told me about the wonderful place he had visited before returning to his own country," which is the bare bones of so much Utopian writing, contains no significant transformation or reversal of an initial situation, and as such is arguably a non-story.[13] The lack of tension or contradiction which is typical of Utopian life[14] is reflected in the manner of its presentation, which is consistent but hardly interesting.

The one factor which redeems some Utopian fiction is the ability of certain authors to stand back from their own work, creating an effect of distanciation. There is, however, some dispute as to when this occurs. According to one critic, Thomas More's *Utopia*, and Utopias in general, are characterized by a "desire for credibility" or verisimilitude, whereas for another, the opposite is the case:[15] the cultural references in *Utopia*, for instance (the allusions to Plato's *Republic*), situate the work in a literary tradition, thus reminding us that we are reading a book and not participating in something real. The critic goes on to describe the processes at work in *Utopia* and Utopias:

[Utopia is] a discourse on contemporary historical reality [and] an imaginary construct. Between them there exists no syntactic link, but they are juxtaposed paratactically. Reading consists in following successively these parallel lines while maintaining their separateness. . . . The writer's art consists in inviting, through a particular treatment of language, a paranoid reading, or in maintaining, through the use of stylistic devices to create distanciation, the schizoid nature of the construction.[16]

By "paranoid" and "schizoid" no pejorative meaning is intended. The words are used to denote, respectively, the confusion of the two levels (the discourse on history and the fictional discourse), and the maintenance of their separation for the purpose of distanciation. If both levels are kept separate, then the play of irony (self-irony; irony at the reader's expense) becomes possible and a kind of safety valve is created through which some of the text's seriousness and didacticism máy escape. The distinction between "paranoid" and "schizoid" writing is a valuable one, in spite of the terminology, and we shall return to it in connection with Fourier.

These remarks on Utopia should be complemented by the reminder of its overlap with other genres, and by a brief mention of its history. For if the genre can be said to have begun "officially" with More's *Utopia*, it is quite possible to work back from the features we have assembled and to discern certain origins, even a kind of prehistory. Thus certain writings of Plato, notably *The Republic*, *Timaeus* and *Critaeus*, might qualify as Utopias, although the first named is really a kind of legislative project. Certainly by the Renaissance it is possible to define a Utopian genre, characterized by a powerful anthropocentrism. The eighteenth century was the heyday of Utopias, for the most part unimaginative and boring, which celebrated the sovereignty of nature (*natura naturans*) and reason. For early nineteenth century Utopias, reason, progress, science, and social emancipation became the main preoccupations. Instead of being isolated spatially — a faraway island — Utopia is now placed in the (not-too-distant) future, and, as such, overlaps with or turns into science fiction. In more modern times, "counter-Utopias" or accounts of Utopia gone wrong (Aldous Huxley, Orwell, Boulle) have become common, continuing a vein which probably had its most illustrious representative in Jonathan Swift. Nevertheless, the need to believe, against all hope, in a perfect future society is still there, especially among the young. Was it not the students of May 1968 who restored Fourier's statue to its pedestal in the Place Clichy?[17]

II *Fourier and Utopia: General*

The students of May 1968 saw Fourier, as did Marx, as a Utopian Socialist, without attaching to the label the critical nuance intended by the German thinker. Fourier clearly does belong to that generation of writers marked by the events of 1793 and determined that things should and could be better, and he has much in common — except his genius — with contemporaries such as Saint-Simon, Leroux, Cabet, Enfantin, Victor Considerant, and a dozen others.[18] But what concerns us here is a more general question: to what extent is Fourier's work assimilable to Utopia as we have described it?

The similarities between Fourier's presentation of life in

Harmony and Utopia are considerable. Everything and everyone is accounted for and classified, each day organized down to the last minute, every desire fitted in with ("enmeshed with") every other desire. The proper functioning of one part of the system is guaranteed by and guarantees the functioning of the rest. Fourier prefers the hierarchical approach to the uniform one, and there are still social classes in Harmony, but there is no possibility of any tension between classes or for their order to be modified or reversed. The family unit is not so much abolished as divested of any real importance, so that it cannot interfere with the serial functioning of society. The careful organization of the Harmonians' daily timetable effectively "purifies" time: "there is never lost time in Harmony" (Xa, 95). Like many Utopian writers, Fourier is very aware of the disorder of nature, preferring to modify it in various ways.[19] Harmony is perfect and nothing is allowed to disturb its perfection.

In what we have called the moral and political domains there are both similarities and differences. Pedagogy is of great importance to Fourier, who believes that every citizen should develop his potential through being useful to the community. Although there are important "religious" institutions — or more correctly, functions — in Harmony, Fourier's concept of religion is such that the inverted commas are needed; gastronomic sainthood really does have very little (or too much?) to do with sainthood in the Christian sense. In general, Fourier's work lacks any real religious sentiment, although it is informed by a very real understanding of the human need to venerate or to be admired within some kind of ritual framework. Hence the extraordinary proliferation of saintly or heroic beings and couples in Harmony and the distribution of honors and recompenses to all and sundry. As for the fear of death which is so powerful in Western society, Fourier, like other Utopian writers, attempts to dispose of it by pretending that death does not exist. In case this is not enough, his cosmology includes a detailed plan of metempsychosis which, as we have seen, accounts for reentry into this life far more satisfactorily than departure from it.[20]

The economics of the Phalanx are, broadly speaking, those of traditional Utopia. Fourier's disdain of money is nowhere more apparent than in his description of Little Hordes' public remuneration of a series which has complained about its share at the annual dividend distribution ceremony, and of the series' shame at being paid in this manner. "This corporation is the one that must control *the great master of the world*, THE VILE METAL named *silver*. The Little Hordes are the universal antidote to cupidity" (V, 146, Fourier's capitalization and italics). Fourier's hatred of commerce is too evident for us to insist further on it; while the basically agricultural — and oral — organization of the Phalanx should also need no further comment.

Thus, if Utopia is "a global, societary project of radical opposition to the dominant order"[21] or the description of an imaginary community, of its economic, moral, and social organization, which is seen as a desirable ideal,[22] then Harmony must qualify for membership of the League of Ideal Communities. The trouble with such definitions is of course their brevity, and the dissimilarities between Harmony and the kind of composite Utopia we have described are so great as to render the membership problematic.

To begin with, various aspects of Harmony are really reversals of standard Utopian features. Although there is no governmental or judicial apparatus in Fourier's community, there is, we have seen, a very elaborate ritual system of a "religious" nature, which complements a detailed educational program for the young. Yet there is arguably a very major element of burlesque in the former, while the latter lacks any kind of administrative framework, has no full-time educators, and neatly solves the school-building problem by having no schools. To take another example: certain Utopias are modeled on the cosmos, because of its perfect, atemporal nature. Nothing happens in the cosmos, or, as Jacques Derrida would put it, it is always already there. Gilles Lapouge is therefore led to write in his book on Utopias: "Can one imagine a god changing from time to time, under the pressure of events, the trajectory of Mercury or the rings of Saturn?"[23] The answer to this apparently rhetorical question is that no god acts in this way, just a man called Charles Fourier, whose cosmos is modeled on Harmony, and "corrected" accordingly. Again, although traditional Utopia knows no future, since there is no way in which perfection can develop, Fourier manages to reconcile perfection, decline, and development in his version of the past and future history of the world. Harmony will eventually deteriorate, during the "descending vibration," until, after 80,000 years, the animal and vegetable world, and eventually the earth, will die. But as the souls of the dead will become united with the great soul of our planet, which will then begin its long, possibly endless ascent of the ladder of creation, its — and our — future is indeed "open."

There are various other relatively minor dissimilarities: Fourier is unique among Utopian writers in recognizing the existence of filth, and one of the very few who do not abolish private property (although no details of the Phalansterians' possessions are ever revealed). The major points of difference are all concerned in one way or another with the extent to which Fourier's writings transgress the static, centric nature of literary or nonliterary Utopia. Above all, the delicate relationship between the individual and society seems to operate to the mutual advantage of both in Fourier, even though the mode of its operation leads to potential problems.

III   *The Individual and Society*

In most ways, Fourier's theory of social relationships is very convincing, since it appears to function solely on the basis of the individual's desires or passions. In Utopia, the control of social mores is effected because a norm has been established; whatever does not conform is therefore deviant, and must be suppressed. Most Utopias, we have suggested, are highly restrictive, with the restrictiveness sometimes being camouflaged by the inhabitants' supposed natural docility and abstemiousness. With Fourier, it is not laws which govern behavior, but behavior which demands that a mechanism be invented to allow everybody to do as they please in a socially useful way. The mechanism is of course the serial organization of work and pleasure. It is because the Phalanx is a "space for encounters," which occur as a result of the interplay of the three distributive passions: the cabalistic, the butterfly, and the composite or enthusiastic, that the kind of classification Fourier devises becomes a framework within which an infinity of social permutations is possible. For classification can either immobilize, or it can free — for what Fourier calls "engrenage" (enmeshing or intermeshing). If the inhabitant of Harmony is a cog in a machine, he is an unusual one, since it is basically he who decides where he will belong or enmesh, and "belonging" is not confined to one group, but up to fifty. Membership of a group or series depends solely on individual inclination, and in one's choice the attractiveness of one's companions, as well as one's work, counts for a great deal. We are a long way from the asceticism and chilly moral concern of so many Utopias.

It is the integration of "maniacs" that poses problems, however. This is effected, we may remember, by education, so that even the Neros of this world become socially useful (VI, 170). In the case of Nero, Fourier argues that his bloodthirstiness will be recognized at a tender age. When he is three he will be put to work in a butchers' group, so that by the time he is twenty, he can be a master butcher. But he will also perform many other tasks, which, along with the art of butchery, will enable him to develop into a useful citizen: "Little by little he will find himself initiated into all branches of learning as the sole result of penchants which Civilization treats as corrupt and which are repressed in children" (Xb, 133). In Civilization, Nero would — and did — simply exercise his bloodthirsty inclinations as soon as he grew up. They would be temporarily hidden and then reappear in a dangerous form (ibid., pp. 133-34).

But how is Nero's bloodthirstiness recognized? Nowhere does Fourier tell us, for the process of recognition has been supplanted by the far more useful one of *prediction*. In a section entitled "On Methodical Horoscopes, or the Calculation of Echos of Manias," Fourier develops what he claims is a far more sophisticated method of predicting what a child may become than the traditional determination of his temperament. Just to have a description of, for instance, a "sanguine" type is useless, since there are hundreds of millions of them. We should therefore focus on the very rare, such as the heel-scratchers, asking ourselves which of the 810 temperaments is dominant, which of the personality types, and which manias (i.e., other than heel-scratching) occur most frequently among them. When seven consecutive generations have been studied, we should be able to determine the correspondences or echoes of the mania in question in the material and passional domains; for instance, if the heel-scratchers predominate among those with temperament number 360 and character number 240, then it is reasonable to predict that a child of seven, in whom this combination is present, will develop the mania by the time he is thirty. If we can predict the minutest mania, we shall have no trouble in determining much more common character traits. We can therefore predict our future Homers, Demosthenes, and

Neros, concludes Fourier, which would have been an immense advantage for the Romans, who would have taken measures to keep the last named from the throne which was not his by right (VII, 394-98).

Now it is one thing to remark that the infant Nero would be encouraged to watch butchers at work, and quite another to envisage the setting-up of what amounts to a global card-index system which would facilitate the integration of potential social undesirables. But the one thing leads to the other. . . . The ultimate arbiter of what is socially desirable is Fourier, who usually seems to be saying that everything is, provided it harms nobody. One merely canalizes the potentially dangerous, turning Nero into a butcher. But it is the apparatus of prediction that allows this to occur, just as the temperamental and sexual compatibilities of host and visiting Harmonians are partly determined by information that is *already* "on file" (XIb, 26). The danger is obvious, and suggests just how close to the horrors of *1984* the fantasy and humor of the *New Amorous World* can come.

But yet again, it is probably Fourier's own lack of total control that prevents Harmony from turning into the world of Orwell. As we saw in the last chapter, the basic principles underlying Fourier's analogical practice are clear enough, but the practice itself is rather blurred. The same applies to Fourier's world of social relationships. Not only are endless permutations possible, but some are clearly outside the system as it was initially envisaged. Fourier's notebooks contain page after page of (unfinished) calculations relating to various kinds of series: "free," "measured," "potential," "contiguous," "compound," "grafted," and so on.[24] These are complemented by page after page of equally unfinished calculations attempting to define the total range of affinities and antipathies *within* each series (XIb, 22-90). Such a debauch of calculations is, we believe, not just doodling, but an attempt to contain the uncontainable, the countless impulses of desire. The dream of a card index of manias may be a totalitarian one, but it may also be born of a kind of despair — possibly a joyous one—before the immense field of desire that Fourier had uncovered.[25]

IV   Space

Harmonian space is radically different from normal Utopian space. Whereas the basic organization of the latter emphasizes centrality and the opposition: inside/outside,[26] for the inventor of Harmony, the opposition is rendered meaningless by his concept of the "place." Fourier's space is "open," with the inhabitants of one Phalanx in contact with those of others, thanks to the encouragement of travel and social intercourse on a global scale. The "raw" space immediately surrounding the Phalanx is redisposed by the practice of serial agriculture, which again facilitates encounter at the level of the individual and the group. Conversely, "intermediate" space, or the vast distances the industrial bands and others have to cover between Phalanxes, is annulled by the lack of any description of the journeys themselves. The road to Utopia, on the other hand, is normally long and of extreme difficulty, as Voltaire's *Candide* testifies.

The road to Utopia also leads to one place. For although Utopia is nowhere, nowhere is only amorphous in the sense that it is contrasted with known space. It is, moreover, singular, in that the ideal city or realm is contrasted with the plurality of known realms or cities, being by definition a focal point of perfection. But Fourier's Utopia proliferates, and the point is no longer focal, but *relational*. Starting with the city itself, Fourier is concerned with one thing only: the facilitation of "association" or communication. Existing cities are rebuilt (IV, 296-313), the monopoly of Paris is consistently attacked and decentralization urged (III, 429-31), and the world's climate improved so that deserts are abolished, rendering every part of the globe fit for human habitation. In Harmony, a network of Phalanxes, united by good roads and regular, comfortable transport, covers the entire globe. Nor is Harmony confined to our planet, for it is transported by our souls to the universes they colonize, which are then modified in accordance with the design of Harmony on earth. Fourier's Utopia, like God, is nowhere. . . and everywhere.

V   Presentation

It is in the presentation of Harmony that Fourier differs most strikingly from other Utopian writers. The Utopian discourse is either fictional (with social, political, or moral overtones) or non-fictional, in which case it is a kind of treatise, whereas the peculiarity of Fourier's work is that it is indiscriminately fictional and nonfictional, with the boundary between the two modes constantly being crossed.

The narrative/descriptive process in (a) More's *Utopia* — which is basically a work of fiction — might be represented as follows, in terms of its verisimilitude:

(a)   *More's View*

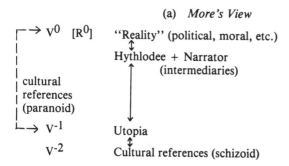

Each level represents a different degree of verisimilitude (V^0, V^{-1}, V^{-2}), with the narrator and the second narrator (Hythlodee) acting as intermediaries between V^0 and V^{-1} and thus increasing the effect of "vraisemblance" or verisimilitude (represented by the dotted line). The degree of verisimilitude will also be affected by the significance one attaches to the cultural references (e.g., to Plato's *Republic*); it will probably be seen as decreased if their literary status is stressed (i.e., *Utopia* is just another text). Conversely, it is likely to be increased if they are taken as part of the reader's cultural heritage, thereby reinforcing the kind of expectations he has about More's book.[27] In the first instance, *Utopia* tends toward the "schizoid," in the second, it would be basically "paranoid."

When we come to Fourier, the process is far more complex, and we have represented it in two parts, (b) and (c), the first as Fourier saw it, and the second as our attempt to account for its actual complexity:

(b) *Fourier's View*

$R^0 + V^0$ "Reality" ("Civilization" + Fourier's view of past
                    history) ↑
                         vs.

$R^0 + V^0$ Fourier (commentator, narrator + narrated life)
                         ↓

$R^0 + V^0$ Harmony (Phalanx; New Amorous World; Cosmogony
                    + future history)

Fourier is the sole intermediary or guarantor of the reality of
everything; the system is paranoid (in both the special and the
normal senses) since reality (R^0) has the same status in all cases.
The problem of verisimilitude is in effect nonexistent.

(c) *Our View*

$R^0 + V^0$ "Reality" (the world as we normally understand it;
                    ↑   Fourier's life insofar as we know about it)

                 Fourier (commentator, narrator + narrated life [V^{-1}]

R^{-1} Phalanx (e.g., education, industrial series, Phalanstery)

V^{-1} Illustrations of life on a Phalanx (e.g., Mondor, Lucas,
                    et al.)

V^{-2} New Amorous World (e.g., episode of Fakma)

V^{-3} Cosmogony and "history" (e.g., VII, 464-96)

The continuous line indicates that the description of the Phalanx can
be considered as a kind of treatise-cum-critique having the hypo-
thetical status (R^{-1}). The dotted lines serve the same purpose as in
(a). No line has been shown linking V^{-3} with V^0, since verisimilitude
has, we believe, to all intents and purposes disappeared. Fourier's
narrated life has been given the status V^{-1} because of its written—
and possibly invented—nature. What complicates (c) is the fact
that, for instance, the New Amorous World (V^{-2}) consists not only
of the episode of Fakma, but a commentary on the episode which
could be assimilated to modern psychoanalytical theory. Yet again,
we are faced with the kind of imbroglio described in our first
chapter.

Such a muddle may have one advantage for the reader, however.
If the dominant mode of presentation for Utopia is the descriptive,

with all the drawbacks that entails, Fourier's "disjointed" writing escapes the danger of sameness in description. Life on a Phalanx, including details of education, the industrial series, and so on, is both described and narrated, with the numerous little stories about pea-sorting, the rivalries of the cabbage- and radish-growers (IV, 496-97), or the solving of the servant problem (IV, 529), relieving the potential monotony. Moreover, Fourier's Utopia is not limited to the Phalanx. It is also a New Amorous World which ultimately encompasses the universe; in his writings on cosmogony and Love, the narrative mode is frequent and the descriptive mode fantastic. One of the reproaches frequently leveled at Utopia is that it has produced no masterpieces, and among the reasons may be its mainly descriptive and moralizing nature.[28] When all the comparisons have been made, it is Fourier's imaginative power that informs both description and narration in his work, leaving most Utopias — and a great deal of non-Utopian writing — far behind.

VI   *Brownian Movement*[29]

Reading Fourier is always a disturbing process, and reading him in the context of Utopian fiction is rather like one's first reading of Robbe-Grillet after a diet of Balzac. In a way, everything we expect is there: the ideal community, the classification and establishment of hierarchies, the reconciliation of individual and collective wellbeing, the emphasis on pedagogy, and so on. But if most of the major tendencies — or dangers — of Utopia are present in Fourier's work, they are present in such a way that repetition becomes proliferation, sameness turns into difference, the focal becomes relational, and out of stasis emerges movement. This is sometimes, we have suggested, in spite of the author, whose system was meditated and worked out with infinite care but insufficient knowledge or logic (e.g., the analogies), and then meddled with incessantly (e.g., the series) by a man who could leave *nothing* alone. Changing the normal order of two frequently coupled adverbs, we might say that Fourier's system *always almost* works. Putting it another way, if we see him as the mad inventor, he is also a not very competent handyman or "bricoleur," as the French say.

How then can we best describe this system, in which the ten-

dency towards stasis, concentration, centrality, and even totalitarianism is ultimately outweighed by proliferation, "play" or
uncertainty, a general dynamism,[30] and — we think — an intermit-
tent ability to stand back and not take one's creation too seriously?
Gilles Lapouge sees the constant travel and encounters in Harmony
in a slightly different way than ourselves. For him, the "clôture"
or closed space of the ideal city has been exchanged for "an
infinity of enclosures," with the ultimate one being the Harmonian universe. But it is a rather special enclosure, which is perhaps
not far removed in essence from the "open" space we have tried
to describe:

Certainly the cities, the desires, and the inventions know no bounds, but
at the same time, as their proliferation is infinite, as the universe is filled
with all the manias, the intense, restless Brownian movement with which
Fourierist society is imbued is simultaneously expanding and closed —
rather like the physical universe whose limits are continuously set by its
own expansion.[31]

CHAPTER 9

Influences on Fourier
and Impact on Posterity

I The Problem of Influence

THE assessment of a writer's impact on posterity and his debt
to his predecessors is a difficult task, since a text is always to a
greater or lesser extent independent of an author's intentions — as
far as these can be known with any certainty — and because what
might be called its general autonomy is also a very doubtful proposition. It is not just a question of an *author* being consciously or
unconsciously influenced by other writers, rather the extent to
which the text itself is a kind of meeting-point or crossroads for
other (implicit) texts. As a recent French critic puts it, texts are
"traversed by" (and traverse) all kinds of other texts.[1] In other
words, when we are reading Fourier, we are also in a sense reading
Rousseau and the Marquis de Sade, and — situated as we are in
the latter part of the twentieth century — Freud and Marx. Because of these interferences, prior to, contemporary with and
subsequent to the "focal" text, some of which are deliberate (for
example, when the author does actually quote or parody another
writer), most of which are not (because they often post-date the
text), the importance of influence implied by traditional studies,
and its "one-way" nature, are notions of both a limited and a
problematic nature.

With Fourier, the question is further complicated by our almost
total lack of precise knowledge about what he actually read. The
findings of a detailed study of his sources by Hippolyte Bourgin
are largely negative: Fourier had neither the means nor the leisure
to study after he left school, and his knowledge was largely
second-hand. He read newspaper accounts of philosophical and
social doctrines rather than the original works; his theories were
complete far too early for contemporaries such as the Owenites or

the Saint-Simonians to have any real effect on them; many of the ideas in his writings were "in the air" at the time rather than culled from specific writers;[2] above all, his originality was so powerful that it tended completely to subsume any "influences." A more recent critic has contested these findings, claiming that Fourier was better informed than has been thought, but with very little supporting evidence.[3] On the rare occasion when Bourgin's hyper-prudence admits to a similarity of ideas — between Fourier and an obscure writer called L'Ange — it is on the basis of a text which turns out to have no real bearing on Fourier's doctrines at all. In addition, it is certain that Bourgin could not have read it.[4]

Such are the pitfalls encountered by those critics whom the French call, with a certain degree of irony, "sourciers" ("sourcer-ers"). Bourgin ends up by implying that Fourier read nothing, which is clearly an exaggeration. But there is some evidence that he read very much at second hand. As we know, he claimed to despise writers and thinkers who had preceded him, consigning Condillac, Newton, Owen, Rousseau, Voltaire and others to a kind of intellectual garbage-heap.[5] It is therefore rare to find in his writings such generous praise as that of Senancour's *Rêveries sur la nature primitive de l'homme*, "[which] I have not read . . . but of which the following extracts have been sent to me. . ." (VII, 421), which is a splendidly ingenuous warning to source-hunters. For this kind of reason — and the others given at the beginning of this chapter — what follows is more of an intellec-tual "situation" of Fourier than a study of influences. It is above all an invitation to discover what other texts can profitably be made to "traverse" the focal text. To read Fourier in the context of later writers: Freud, Marx, Raymond Roussel, André Breton, or Johan Huizinga — and the reverse — is not to devalue him or them, nor should it necessarily demonstrate the priority or superiority of anybody. The aim of this kind of intertextual reading is rather to develop an interplay of meaning that should enhance all the works involved. Where Fourier's predecessors or contemporaries are concerned, it is our knowledge of them rather than him that is likely to be enhanced by comparison, the strangeness of his works highlighting certain tendencies which he may well have inherited, but which he then pushed to their limit.

II *Fourier, the Enlightenment, and Romanticism*

Fourier lived through eight regimes and the transition from the Enlightenment to Romanticism, known as pre-Romanticism. From the Enlightenment he may well have derived his optimistic belief in the use of Reason as the means of transforming all aspects of life, his search for mathematical or geometrical laws which would govern the four "movements," his muted deism, and his insistence on happiness as the goal of human existence.[6] He also probably owed certain less intellectual features of his work to the aristo-cratic eighteenth century: "his taste for refinement, elegance, fine music, and elaborately orchestrated sexual and gastronomic experiences."[7] His obvious enjoyment of intellectual discussion is also a trait of the Enlightenment, even if it did not lead to the kind of intellectual friendships that were so common in the eigh-teenth century. In his correction of nature in the interests of improving the world's climatic system, and the general agricultural bias of Harmony, he belongs to an age that had little time for nature as the Romantics were to see it, and has certain affinities with the Physiocrats.[8]

One of the many paradoxes of Fourier is that a writer who stressed the power of Reason should have seen Man as a funda-mentally irrational being[9] and then taken that irrationality as a basis for his optimism. Fourier, like Rousseau, believes that humanity is naturally good, and again like Rousseau, the Pre-Romantics, and the Romantics, emphasizes the quality of sensibil-ity which makes Man interesting — and also potentially vulnerable to himself and to others. The wave of sensibility which swept Europe from the mid-eighteenth century on, the cult of the un-fortunate hero or heroine (Werther, Clarissa Harlowe, Adolphe, and many others), and the emphasis on melancholy and death, produced several great aberrations, among them the Marquis de Sade and Charles Fourier. For both, the role of the passions and hence sexuality was primordial: the sexual drive was present in Man, and it was therefore to be explored to the full. For the former, the exploration led to a fascination with evil and death, to the bizarre Utopia of the castle of Silling (*The 120 Days of Sodom*) with its gigantic, somber, and repetitive sodomistic and copro-phagic orgy, which few participants survived. For the latter, the exploration led to the Phalanx and a more varied and joyous sexuality celebrating the diversity and creativity of mankind, and ending, not in death, but in a renewed life on another plane.

When the French Romantic movement had established itself, a very important current of "Social Romanticism" emerged, embodied in what have been called "secular religions,"[10] and turning the system-seeking tendencies of the Enlightenment into system-inventing: the need for a total explanation of the world belongs to the restless intellectual nature of the Romantic spirit.[11] More specific reasons for this proliferation of socioreligious theories include a disenchantment with the aftermath of the French Revolution and a concomitant desire for social unity based on a solid theoretical foundation; a resurgence of religious belief; and, along with this resurgence, a kind of ground-swell of all kinds of basically mystic thought: Swedenborgianism, Theosophy, Rosicrucianism, Freemasonry, and various other doctrines that normally go under the general heading of Illuminism or Occultism. To the social, mystic, or Illuminist tendencies should be added a belief in science, human perfectibility, and indefinite progress that culminated in Victor Hugo's vision, in the poem "Plein Ciel," of the "aéroscaphe" or aerial ship symbolizing Man's ascent toward perfection. The proportion of religious, scientific, and social thought varies according to the system, but all are more or less Utopian. Chronologically, Fourier and Saint-Simon vie for priority, since the adumbration of the former's theories can be found in the "Letter to the High Judge" of 1803, the year in which Saint-Simon's first book, the *Lettres d'un habitant de Genève*, was published. Neither Etienne Cabet nor Proudhon was first published until the 1840s, while Robert Owen's *A New View of Society* appeared in 1814.

The theories of Fourier and Saint-Simon offer in any case some striking dissimilarities, particularly in the realm of religion. Whereas Fourier uses God as a reference-point only, Saint-Simon is obsessed by religious problems, founding a new religion, with its own special form of worship, priesthood, and theology. Needless to say, there were some interesting schisms among his followers, some of whom, led by one Prosper Enfantin, founded a community at Ménilmontant in 1832, which was rapidly dissolved by the authorities on the grounds that it offended against public morality. Saint-Simon's plan for a government of scientists and industrialists, and his insistence on the industrial rather than the agricultural development of society are also radically different from Fourier's concept of a new social order. What they have in common — the belief in association, a concern for the poor, the search for a new morality, and a contempt for the parasitical layers of society — is so general as to render the search for any priority of thought meaningless. The most specific similarity is probably their common reference to Newton as a precursor of their theories.

The question of Fourier's Illuminism is far more difficult to resolve. That there are similarities between various important aspects of his thought and widespread Illuminist doctrines is certain. In general, the Illuminists held that Man, who had emanated from God, had fallen from Grace and was living in a state of evil, equated with our material existence (Hugo's famous "matter is evil"). Eventually Mankind will be redeemed, after a long series of reincarnations. To this was added, largely through the spread of Swedenborg's thought, the belief that the material world was a pale reflection of the spiritual world, but related to it through a series of symbols or "correspondences" which needed to be deciphered.[12] In France, the works of Illuminists or Occultists such as Emmanuel Swedenborg (1688-1772), Martinez Pasqualis (c. 1715-1779), Louis de Saint-Martin (1743-1803), Lavater (1741-1801), and Mesmer (1734-1815) were widely read, having a lasting impact on many of the most important literary writers of the early and mid-nineteenth century, notably Balzac and Hugo.

For some years at the turn of the century, Fourier had lived in or near Lyons, which was at that time one of the most important "mystic" centers of France,[13] and it was inevitable that he should have come into contact there with the major aspects of Illuminist thought. The most important is obviously the doctrine of "correspondences," although the mystic, theocentric aspects of Swedenborg's beliefs were far removed from his own anthropocentric turn of mind. As for the doctrines of reincarnation and metempsychosis that were central to Illuminism, they had been part of many religions for thousands of years. In other words, although it is likely that Fourier was marked by Illuminist thought, the Illuminists in turn are marked by traditions that go back to Plato and beyond: for instance, Swedenborg's "correspondences" are a variant on Plato's theory of ideas.[14] No precise influence on Fourier's thought by the Illuminists alone can thus be determined. As Hubert Juin remarks, in a study of Fourier's "presence" in modern poetry, they form an "undeniable background," but no more.[15]

There are, however, two writers, one of whom is in the mainstream of Illuminism, the other outside, who do offer some important parallels with Fourier. The first is the strange Restif de la Bretonne (1734-1806), a very prolific novelist who combines fantasy, a primitive kind of science fiction, and social criticism in various works. *Le Pornographe* (1769) is concerned with the rehabilitation of prostitutes, seeking to show that they have social utility and professional dignity. *La Découverte australe par un homme volant* (1781: republished in 1977) and the *Lettres du tombeau ou les Posthumes* (1802) both develop what has been called a "vitalist cosmogony,"[16] while *Les vingt Epouses des vingt associés* (1780) is a kind of social Utopia situated in France. The first- and last-named offer only very general similarities with Fourier, whose rehabilitation of prostitution is achieved by the imaginative, pseudoreligious institution of Angelic Couples, whereas Restif's is very prosaic in comparison. Restif's social Utopia is also quite different from the Phalanx in its banishment of luxury and its muted, moralizing nature.

Restif's cosmogony is, however, remarkably like Fourier's in its general outlines, although the detail differs. Our planet will have a new life after it has dissolved in the sun; planets live, die, and copulate with one another and possibly with themselves: "perhaps the suns have two sexes between them or is every sun androgynous?"; when our earth acquires a second satellite new animal species will be created; our souls transmigrate; God is related to the sun.[17] The most obvious difference is the theocentric nature of Restif's universe and the importance of what amounts to sunworship. In themselves, the various aspects of Restif's cosmogony are not particularly unusual, and can be found elsewhere in Illuminist writings. But when they are brought together in a single work which antedates by a few years Fourier's writings in which the same ideas are found, then on this occasion there does seem a high probability of influence.

The second writer is Bernardin de Saint-Pierre, whose complete works were edited by one Aimé Martin, the husband of Bernardin's widow. From 1813 to 1830, Martin was on friendly terms with Fourier. The editorial comments on the volume of the complete works containing Bernardin's *Harmonies de la nature* (first published in 1815) are markedly Fourierist in tone, and the *Harmonies* themselves — and earlier *Etudes de la nature* (1784) — are basically a compendium of analogies (a word which in Bernardin is interchangeable with harmony).

The analogies in the *Harmonies* extend to all domains: the vegetable, celestial, physical, and the moral, while harmonies from one domain are linked with and explain those from another: Bernardin takes the example of wheat from the vegetable domain, for example, and draws analogies between its properties and the features of other domains. Among the hundreds of analogies developed or suggested are those between: the inhabitants of the four parts of the earth and the four divisions of the animal kingdom (e.g., "Black Africans are robust like quadrupeds"); flowers and stars; the earth and the human body (e.g., the distribution of hair on the human body and the earth's vegetation); metals and planets; the four ages of Man and the four parts of the globe. The final book of the *Harmonies* contains a homage — with some reservations — to Newton, followed by a description of the "Harmonies of the Heavens and the Worlds" including accounts of life on other planets and many more analogies between planetary and other domains.[18] Here, as elsewhere in Bernardin, the triviality of most analogies is rather depressing. Fourier's may be occasionally tedious, but they are never banal.

It thus seems possible that the idea of a developed system of analogies was suggested to Fourier either by direct acquaintance with Bernardin's work or by what he had been told of it. Possibly Bernardin acted as a kind of intermediary between Fourier and Swedenborg, in the sense that the last-named theorized "correspondences" of a basically mystic nature, while the first-named provided examples, still within the framework of a religious view of the universe, but attended by less overt Illuminism. But in neither case, nor in the case of Restif, nor indeed of any other writer, is the influence sufficient for us to be able to say that Fourier's work is directly tributary to theirs. Even if it were, we are not sure precisely what his work would have "lost" or "gained." The interest of such speculation lies far more in the light it may shed on intellectual history in general than in the curious process of accretion to or erosion of an author's "originality" that it sometimes informs.

III   *Fourier and Posterity: Literature*

The impact of Fourier's writings on nineteenth-century literature appears to have been limited. Most people thought, with no little justification, that he was mad, and if Stendhal, Michelet, George Sand, and Béranger expressed mingled interest and skepticism, writers such as Flaubert and Louis Reybaud were openly hostile, the former ridiculing Fourier in *Bouvard et Pécuchet*,[19] and the latter in *Jérôme Paturot*. The Parnassian poet Leconte de Lisle wrote several poems of Fourierist inspiration, although it sometimes coexisted uneasily with subject matter from Antiquity: the poem "Niobé," of Hellenic inspiration, had a Fourierist ending tacked on and then subsequently amputated. Zola wrote one late novel, *Travail*, with a definite Fourierist flavor (although he appears to have known Fourier only at second hand), in which, as its title partly indicates, the value of work and the vital importance of man's passions are celebrated.[20] Until recently it was thought that there were virtually no other Fourierist plays, poems, or novels in the nineteenth century except those, of dubious literary merit, produced by disciples, or disciples of disciples. These are very large in number, but no detailed study of them has yet been undertaken, although its historical interest would be considerable. On the other hand, the moment that one poses the existence of disciples, there is a high probability of a permeation of Fourier's ideas.

Thus, for some years, an Australian scholar, Peter Hambly, has been reexamining the work of many nineteenth-century poets in the light of this assumption, and has come up with some surprising and convincing results. He has shown, for instance, that the influence of Fourierism in Leconte de Lisle's work is far more extensive than is normally supposed, and that even poets so apparently hostile or indifferent as Théophile Gautier or Théodore de Banville are by no means untouched by Fourier's doctrines and terminology. Above all, he has demonstrated beyond all reasonable doubt the presence of Fourierism in Baudelaire's work.

Baudelaire alludes to Fourier only twice in his published writings (both times along with Swedenborg), as being one of the initiators of the theory and practice of "analogies" or "correspondences," but calls him "pompous." A letter to the Fourierist Alphonse Toussenel, written in 1856, the year before the publication of *Les Fleurs du mal*, claims that Fourier's importance is grossly overrated: we know instinctively, and through the poets, that Nature is an allegory, writes Baudelaire.[21] In spite of these reservations, Baudelaire's poems are full of Fourierist commonplaces, while certain lines of some of his most famous poems ("L'Invitation au voyage," "Le Voyage," "Le Cygne") derive from the Fourierist press, for instance. One of the most vexed questions in Baudelaire studies, the architecture of *Les Fleurs du mal,* is also reopened by Hambly, who claims very plausibly that it owes a good deal to Fourier's writings on series.[22]

Fourier's direct influence on modern poetry is very slight, since it is only since the reprinting of the so-called complete works, with additions, by Editions Anthropos (1966-1968) that he has been accessible. He was discovered in 1940 by André Breton, who found his works a revelation — of himself — and wrote a long *Ode à Charles Fourier*, published in 1947.[23] Breton apart, it is hard to find a modern poet whose work betrays an awareness of Fourier's work, or a conscious attempt at imitating his analogical practice. For this reason, the poet-critic Hubert Juin justly writes not of Fourier's influence on modern poetry, but of his "presence," which he attributes to an "extremely fruitful 'occultation,'" assuring Fourier an almost involuntary posterity, so that he seems to have disappeared from everything, whereas he is present everywhere."[24] Fourier's concepts, continues Juin, making the same point as ourselves, insinuated themselves everywhere in the nineteenth century, although no writer accepted them *in toto*. When the Surrealist revolution began, it may therefore have drawn upon many of his ideas, none of which was recognized as such, through very many intermediaries.

The similarities between Fourier and Surrealist thought and practice are considerable. The most important is undoubtedly the desire for a total break (Fourier's "Ecart absolu") with contemporary society, the accepted notion of reality, and established creative practice: the most general problem Surrealism must deal with, wrote Breton in the *Second Manifeste du Surréalisme*, is that of "human expression in all its forms." *Everything* must be changed, and a new moral and social order must be created. The role of woman is one of Surrealism's constant preoccupations, for her emancipation is a *sine qua non* of the kind of moral change envisaged: not only her social but — as a concomitant — her sexual status must be improved, so that she is on a completely equal footing with man. Finally, the fullest development of our imagination is attempted by a process of free association known as automatic writing, whereby — in theory, at least — the Surrealist transcribes what his thoughts or dreams indicate, without any intervention on the part of his reason. The result is sometimes, but not inevitably, the cascade of startling images for which Surrealist poetry is known.

Fourier thought dreams were a waste of time: "Sleep is a simple state in which the body does not obey the soul: it is a separation of body and soul. During sleep the latter lapses into an irrational state and usually has vague thoughts whose absurdity it recognizes upon awakening" (III, 328). For the Surrealists, on the other hand, dreams were the foundation of all experience and the practice of writing as they understood it. No doubt for this reason Breton, as we have seen, contrasted the freedom of Surrealist "metaphor" with the prefabricated ponderousness of Fourier's "analogies."[25] But the variety of Surrealist and quasi-Surrealist practice, and the distinction we have tried to draw between "primary" and "secondary" analogies in Fourier's work — the first basically arbitrary and the second motivated by often doubtful logic — should permit the kind of intertextual reading we have been urging. The examples of Surrealist poetry given by Juin, although they vary enormously, from the apparently systematic to the completely "free," all take on renewed interest, in terms of the procedures involved, when confronted with Fourier's analogies.

If Fourier is "marginal," difficult to fit into any of the usual literary or nonliterary categories, then the same is true of Raymond Roussel (1877-1933). The Surrealists were very interested in him, but the interest was not reciprocated. Not only was he extremely eccentric, but the procedures of literary composition he employed were quite extraordinary. There are basically three: (a) the opening sentence of a text is repeated at the end with one letter changed. The "story" accounts for (or is accounted for by) the change; (b) two nouns are linked by the preposition "à" and then used with different meanings; (c) what Roussel calls his "procédé évolué," or the systematic practice of homophony in works such as *Le Poète et la Moresque* — e.g., "Napoléon, premier empereur" gives "Nappe ollé ombre miettes hampe air heure." Commentators on Roussel — and there have been many in recent years

— are all agreed that this enterprise, and particularly the "evolved" procedure, destroys what might be called our semantic innocence, or the belief that words denote (one) thing(s) in an unambiguous manner.[26] Using basically the same procedure as did Fourier 100 years previously, Roussel opens up the possibilities of language and in particular semantic polyvalence. Words act as generators of other words — and hence of meanings associated with the words generated — in a procedure that is harder to emulate than one might think. The fact that Fourier is a precursor of Roussel is in itself of perhaps minor interest, and it should be stressed that this kind of word play has a long history. But whereas it used to be — and sometimes still is — treated lightly, the tendency is now to take it very seriously indeed, for the reasons given in Chapter 7. Yet again, there is a kind of conjuncture of Fourier and the present which is fruitful, less in the context of any kind of influence, than in the way in which it focuses attention on certain phenomena (here: linguistic) that have interesting and sometimes disturbing implications for us all.

IV   *Fourier and Posterity: Social and Political Thought*

As we indicated in our Preface, we are not attempting a study of Fourierism, or the modifications to Fourier's thought by disciples and its subsequent spread in France and elsewhere. Fourierist communities were widespread in the nineteenth century, particularly in the United States, where no less than thirty-five were founded between 1841 and 1858. Most of them were of very short duration, and the longest only survived for thirteen years.[27] To these should be added various other communities such as Oneida (1848-1880), which offers similarities with the Phalanx without having been inspired by Fourier, or where the inspiration was very indirect.

Fourier's relationship with the cooperative movement, which had its beginnings in Rochdale, England, is similarly indirect. There are of course certain common points, notably Fourier's ardent defense of the consumer, and the fact that he envisaged the formation of various vaguely cooperative organizations such as "communal counters," which would be better than nothing in the event of nobody's financing a trial Phalanx. But it is evident that the movement had stronger connections with Owenism than

Fourierism, and Henri Desroche concludes his detailed study of the cooperative movement's debt to Fourier as follows: "In short, it is less a question of natural progeny than of an adopted Father."[28]

Fourier has also been claimed as a precursor of both anarchism and communism, which is another pointer to the difficulty (or ease) of assimilating such an unusual thinker to any particular movement. Insofar as the Phalanx was a community with no government, wherein each individual developed his full potential without any interference from the collective body, Fourier's system could be called anarchist.[29] On the other hand—and therein lies the uniqueness of Fourier's ideal community—every permutation of desire is facilitated (but not imposed) by a kind of master plan, the serial organization of all activities, which is the detailed counterpart to the general theory of Passionate Attraction. The Phalanx just escapes anarchy on the one hand and totalitarianism on the other, we believe, by virtue of the way in which the exigencies of the individual and those of the community are *harmonized*, with all the implications that word had for Fourier. It also escapes the latter by virtue of the "play" in the system, whereby the "rule of exceptions" is unintentionally complemented by the unfinished nature of Fourier's calculations.

It is to Marx and Engels that we owe the distinction between "scientific" and "Utopian" socialism, and a fascinating discussion of socialism's precursors, in particular Fourier, Saint-Simon, and Robert Owen. Although they classed Fourier as a Utopian Socialist on account of the fantastic vein in his writings, and had various other reservations, Engels in particular held him in very high regard, writing to Marx in the following terms: "I wanted to have Fourier translated by some friends in Bonn . . . leaving aside of course the cosmogonic absurdities—and if the publisher had been in agreement it would have been the first part of the socialist library we were planning to bring out."[30] And if the fantasy was not acceptable, at least the humor was; it was again Engels who, commending Fourier's attack on the structure of contemporary society, contrasted his verve and wit with the arid solemnity of his disciples.[31]

There were obviously both attractive and unattractive features of Fourier's thought for the authors of the *Communist Manifesto*. On the one hand, they praised Fourier's critique of society and in particular his contrast between the slogans of the Enlightenment and the realities of commercial speculation following the Revolution;[32] while Engels believed that Fourier's notion of allowing each individual to discover the task(s) that suited him — and thus allying work and pleasure—was the great axiom of social philosophy.[33] On the other hand, it was Fourier's concept of work—together with his failure to recognize the emergent role of the industrial proletariat and the incipient class struggle—that led to the most serious reservations on the part of Marx in particular.

"Work cannot become a game, as Fourier wished," wrote Marx, who believed that, even in a Communist society, work would require effort.[34] For Marx there was a boundary between productive work and creative activity which could not be crossed, however satisfactory the social organization might become. Both thinkers wanted work to be far more attractive, and production to be the result of freedom instead of coercion. But in Fourier's predominantly agricultural community, with its accent on consumption rather than production and its elaborate system of amusing rituals, "work" has a status that is little short of ludic, and as such is very different from the austere, Marxian activity.[35] Whether this implies a less realistic or less flattering view of human nature than that of Marx, or indeed of most social thinkers, will be discussed in our conclusion.

V   *Fourier and Posterity: Sociopsychological Thought*

Charles Fourier has been seen as a pioneer of enlightened educational thought, as a precursor of the "sexual revolution," and as a Freudian before Freud. All of these claims are more or less true, and are another form of testimony to his "presence" in the modern world.

In the domain of education, many of Fourier's ideas, or extensions of them, are now common currency, and a detailed comparison with those of Jean-Jacques Rousseau would be a worthwhile study—provided it did not lead to the depreciation of the one to the advantage of the other. For both, education deals with children as human beings in their own right, with its goal the development of all aspects of these unique beings. Fourier stresses the social nature of the child and his productive usefulness, whereas Rousseau would have him brought up in isolation by a

tutor, with the occasional visit to workshops as his only initiation
to productive society.[36] It is in particular this emphasis on the
sociality of children and the "open-ness" of the classroom (so
open, we have suggested, that it no longer exists) that render
Fourier's ideas interesting to contemporary educationalists.[37]

In the Phalanx, a child is surrounded from birth by his peers
and by adults not usually related to him, and as he grows up the
enrichment and learning processes become increasingly reciprocal.
Mutual teaching and mutual emulation are encouraged, and
rather than adults setting an example to the children, the reverse
occurs in the case of the "Little Hordes" and their public functions at dividend-distribution time. Many of their other activities
such as road-mending, would today go under the heading of
"Community Service" or its extension, the British "Voluntary
Service Overseas," or the U.S. "Peace Corps." More important,
the combination of education and productive work—even if it
is not begun at the age of two—is widespread, in different forms,
in the Soviet Union and the People's Republic of China, with
Fourier being recognized as a predecessor by Soviet scholars.[38]
Various educational institutions in the Soviet Union in particular
have carried out experiments with a strong Fourierist flavor,
especially the alliance of study and productive work, although
there is no evidence that his ideas are directly responsible for the
curriculum or particular pedagogical practices.[39]

In England, A. S. Neill founded his famous school, Summerhill, on principles very similar to Fourier's: the freedom of
children to choose whatever activity, intellectual or otherwise, that
pleased them; the arranging of activities by a General Assembly,
rather like the "Work Exchange" of Harmony; the importance of
manual and outdoor work; and the role of play as a substitute for
aggression. Being a real establishment, Summerhill was naturally
the kind of compromise between the ideal and practical that is
unknown in Utopia. Children attended it because their parents
could afford to send them there; the problem of their sexual
behavior had to be resolved in terms of expediency vis-à-vis the
outside world; above all, it remained a school, isolated from the
rest of the community. But Summerhill, and the numerous other
"free expression" experiments being conducted in various parts of
the world, all have in common with Fourier the guiding principle
that true creativity and a genuine social awareness can develop

only in a community characterized by a lack of constraint. It is an optimistic view of humanity—and childhood in particular—but it is a respectable one that is far from being disproved.

Fourier's published views on feminism may well be the product of a very illiberal mind; they are nonetheless stirring statements for his time and, taken in the context of his writings on sexual relationships, provide a remarkably modern compendium of ideas. He was taken very seriously by one of the earliest French feminists, Flora Tristan (1803-1844), who used his statement: *"The extension of the privileges of women is the general principle of all social progress"* (I, 133, his italics) as an epigraph for her *L'Emancipation de la femme* (1845). He was also praised for his stand on women's rights by Marx and Engels, who admired an aphorism very similar to the one just quoted (I, 172), and agreed with his view that monogamy and real estate were the main characteristics of Civilization.[40]

Very recently there have been signs that Fourier, as well as being *seen* as one of the precursors of the sexual revolution, is being *exploited* as such (no pejorative sense is intended). In his plea for a lifting of sexual taboos, his implicit assumption that there was no such thing as a sexual norm, and his claim that the marriage relationship is invariably a farce, Fourier anticipated, in a general sense, the freeing of relationships between sexes—and those between members of the same sex. Whether society will ever accept his vision of generalized, decommercialized prostitution celebrated in institutions like the Angelicate or the trials undergone by postulants to Sainthood is doubtful. But it is, it seems, now ready for paperback selections of Fourier's writings on the love relationship: in 1975, Gallimard put out such a volume in its popular "Idées" collection under the title *Charles Fourier: Vers la Liberté en amour* (Toward Freedom in Love). Late in 1977 a work appeared, entitled *Le Nouveau Désordre amoureux* (The New Amorous Disorder),[41] featuring two snowmen in an unambiguous—and very unsnowmanlike—posture on the cover, and was advertised by a quotation from the *Nouveau Monde amoureux.* This is an excellent sign, and bodes well for the future, especially the commercial future of the publisher concerned. The use of Fourier's name for advertising purposes also suggests that he may be becoming better known than our Preface claims.

It is inevitable that Freud's name should be invoked in a discussion of Fourier's analysis of human sexuality. In a very broad sense Fourier's recognition of the importance of the sexual drive is pre-Freudian, and his analysis of manias and the process whereby they are "choked" ("engorgés") is a highly perceptive way of describing what is now known as the mechanism of repression. It has even been claimed that the famous passage on Mme Strogonoff (VII, 391-92), in which a third person advises her of her lesbianism and acts as an intermediary between her and her victim, is a primitive version of the psychoanalytical cure.[42] The difference between Fourier's account of the intervention, which is merely a device to let the reader know what Mme Strogonoff's true passion was, and the rigorous and lengthy practice of the cure, is, however, too great for even a general comparison to be sustained.

As for the mechanism of sublimation, the channeling of pregenital drives into socially approved channels (e.g., members of fire brigades are sublimating their urethral eroticism), its relationship with what Fourier calls "absorbing substitution" ("substitution absorbante," IV, 352-55) is equally doubtful. For sublimation to operate, repression of the pregenital drive has first to occur: one cannot sublimate what has not been repressed. But the widespread use of "absorbing substitution" is contrasted by Fourier with repression (IV, 33); in other words, it does not follow it, but replaces it. For example:

Daphne has been heartbroken since her lover left yesterday. But today if another more handsome and likeable man turns up Daphne will have him, and her grief at Antenor's departure will be absorbed in the charm of a new relationship with Pollux.

This is the true *purgation* of passions: *absorbing substitution.* (IV, 353)

This example and others given by Fourier are also hardly pregenital in character. The term "substitution"[43] would thus be more appropriate today, as in his own time.

But perhaps the most striking difference between Fourier and Freud is the former's refusal to accept the idea of infantile sexuality. Children are a third or "neuter" sex (III, 168), and various means such as the Vestalate are used to postpone the awakening of sexual awareness as long as possible: ideally until they are nineteen or twenty. The only possible exception to this, and one which was certainly not recognized as such by Fourier, is provided by the activities of the Little Hordes, which are of a fairly blatant anal-erotic nature.[44] But in general the contrast with Freud could hardly be greater, largely offsetting the similarities which are of a rather general kind. Fourier's importance for social or psychological thought lies rather, it has been observed, in his profound examination of the "problem of the relationship between man's instinctual life and human society,"[45] with the uniqueness of the solution lying in his refusal to accept any traditional constraints or to invent new ones: society is fashioned by humanity and is the product of its desires. Or, to put it another way, the immense task which Fourier undertook was the provision of a social framework which encouraged the inventiveness of Man's passions. We do not find the framework totally implausible and—more importantly—the insights into social behavior are sometimes quite remarkable. For these reasons, Fourier deserves the respect of posterity.

CHAPTER 10

Conclusion—Fourier's Concept of Man

AS Fourier's main concern was with Man as a social being, we may reasonably ask at the conclusion of this study whether his view of humanity is consistent, and whether it is optimistic or pessimistic. The answer is complex, particularly as his published and private views were informed by paranoia. But if we can put aside motives for a moment, and interrogate the text alone, the picture may be slightly clearer. There are two sides to it: a negative and a positive one.

On the negative side, humanity is seen as naturally good but essentially passive. Fourier's view of Man's degeneration (what he calls the Fall) is that it came about as a result of overpopulation and resultant food shortages, factors over which mankind had very little control. The ensuing social periods are simply different forms of degenerescence, culminating in Civilization, which will stagnate in its current phase—until somebody listens to Charles Fourier. Once the Trial Phalanx has been established by a bene-factor motivated by the prospect of enormous monetary gain, Man's cupidity will ensure that others follow (one should remember the fantastic promises of a mainly financial nature that abound in Fourier's writings). Within the Phalanxes, Man's main irrational impulse, the sexual instinct, will largely determine the structure of society and the pattern of social relationships. These will be facilitated by Fourier's updated version of Juvenal's *Panem et Circenses*, Meat Pies and Parades. The so-called reli-gious trappings and rituals of Harmonian society and the system of universal honors and distinctions have a disturbing ring that is at once military and juvenile.[1]

The picture may be slightly overdrawn, but it is not a cari-cature: Fourier's reconciliation of the Fall with Man's natural goodness, for instance, is at best paradoxical and at worst confused. On the positive side, humanity's passivity is offset by two factors: Fourier's gift of recognizing in the irrational a force that could be harnessed in the interests of social order and individual development; and his vision of mankind "intervening" in the global and, later, the cosmic order. Fourier's anthropocentrism is quite unique in that it has its basis in a vision of Man as simultaneously passive and active, and as a being whose essential goodness is fostered by the encouragement of what are normally regarded as his basest instincts.

There is also another way of looking at the important elements of play in Fourier's ideal society. In the sense that it is first engaged in by children, play is juvenile. But it need not be depreciated by the label. One of the many paradoxes of Fourier is that, while he virtually ignored—or tried to suppress—the importance of infantile sexuality, he designed a society that functioned largely on the basis of the other major characteristic of childhood, its propensity toward play. And play, as various authors from Johan Huizinga to Freud and Norman Brown have demonstrated, is one of the fundamental elements in adult society. Huizinga gives the following as its major characteristics: it is above all a voluntary activity, an expression of our freedom and creative of order; it is closely linked with religion, with art, with ritual, and dramatic or musical performance; it is, or used to be, a major element in war. On the other hand, writes Huizinga, "not being 'ordinary' life, it stands outside the immediate satisfaction of wants and appetites, indeed it interrupts the appetitive process."[2] For this reason, it also needs a closed space.

Perhaps the uniqueness of Fourier's social vision is to have expanded the frontiers of play to include the imperative needs of our appetites, in a gastronomic and sexual sense. The latter sense is certainly suggested by Norman Brown in the concluding chapter of *Life against Death*, entitled "The Resurrection of the Body," which argues for the abolition of repression. "The life instinct, or sexual instinct, demands activity of a kind that, in contrast to our current mode of activity can only be called play," writes Brown, who claims that "to find social theorists who are thinking about the real problems of our age, we have to go back to the Marx of 1844, or even the philosophers influencing Marx in 1844, Fourier and Feuerbach."[3] Curiously enough, sport is not included in the curriculum of Harmonians. The oversight may simply stem from Fourier's nationality. This apart, Harmonian society is pervaded by the play principle. For it is a society without the apparatus of government and bureaucracy, yet dominated by institutions and frequently erotic ritual: the various parades, the "work exchange," the dividend-sharing ceremonies (with the vital role of the Little Hordes), the Courts of Love, the regular operatic performances given in every Phalanx, with the stress put on participation and the public rewarding of champions in all domains of human activity, however trivial some of them may seem to us. Moreover, it is regulated according to the supreme example of elevated play, mathematics: "It [mathematics] unfolds under a rigorously arbitrary, nonutilitarian set of rules. It delineates a privileged area open only to those who understand and observe these rules. Yet any number of new rules can be devised and 'played by.' Mathematics shares with those modes of mental action which Huizinga designates as 'ludic' certain criteria of formal beauty, of difficulty, of profound wit."[4] And if the concept of play is extensible to the domain of human passions, then Fourier's description of them as "animated mathematics" (XIb, 161) becomes even more appropriate.

Charles Fourier has left one of the strangest corpora in French writing. He is a kind of douanier Rousseau of social and political thought and one of the great "marginals" of literature, remarkable for his imaginative power and exasperating on account of his narrow-minded chauvinism, a living exemplar of his own theory of the contact of extremes. We have hesitated to call his work humane, because of its undercurrents of hatred and bigotry, yet it is inspiring and provocative because of the relationship it can be seen to have with some of the most important and contradictory trends in contemporary literature and social thought. If it has been our focal point over the first eight chapters, it is fitting that the ninth and tenth should have led us outward from it to have become "a space for encounters."

Notes and References

All books in French are published in Paris, unless otherwise stated.

Chronology

1. According to his biographer, Charles Pellarin, Fourier dropped the second "r" when he was eighteen.

Chapter One

1. Our main source, and that of all previous critics of Fourier, is Charles Pellarin, *Charles Fourier, sa vie et sa théorie*. We have used the 1843 edition, which is the most complete. Pellarin's admiration for his subject is unlimited (except where Fourier's views on sex are concerned), and the book must therefore be used with great caution.

2. Frank Manuel, *The Prophets of Paris* (Cambridge, Mass., 1962), p. 225.

3. Pascal Bruckner, *Fourier* (1975), p. 7.

4. Simone Debout, Introduction to Charles Fourier, *Théorie des quatre mouvements* (1967), p. 8, n.1.

5. For the historical background, see *Histoire de Lyon et du Lyonnais* (Toulouse, 1975), p. 302.

6. Charles Fourier, *Théorie des quatre mouvements et des destinées générales* (Leipzig [= Lyon]: Pelzin, 1808). This, and subsequent major works have been reprinted by Editions Anthropos, Paris, 1966-1968 (see bibliography for details). All subsequent references to Fourier's works, unless stated, will be to this edition, thus: IX, 154. Volumes X and XI are each in two parts, and will be referred to respectively as Xa, Xb, XIa, XIb.

7. See Chapter 9.

8. See also Pellarin (above, note 1), pp. 244-49; H. Desroche, *La Société festive* (1975), pp. 220-35; a letter by Fourier to an unknown correspondent, complaining of the incompetence of the person who put up the money, one Baudet-Dulary (Paris: Archives Nationales, 10 AS 31); and the circular letter already mentioned (Paris: Institut Français d'Histoire Sociale, 14 AS 2).

9. A favorite phrase of Fourier. See e.g. II, 194; VIII, 264. See also Chapter 2.

10. Nicholas Riasanovsky, *The Teaching of Charles Fourier* (Berkeley, 1969), p. 14.

11. Roland Barthes, *Sade, Fourier, Loyola* (1971), p. 121. Bread is little consumed in Harmony, whereas sugar and sugar-based food abound (e.g., Xa, 159-60).

12. Paris, Archives Nationales, 10 AS 25.

13. *Recueil d'articles extraits de la "Phalange, revue de la Science sociale"* (1849), Part 3, pp. 127-28.

14. "L'Inventeur et son siècle" (The Inventor and His Century) in *La Phalange*, IX (March 1849), 193-240.

15. *Recueil d'articles* (above, note 13), Part 5, p. 9.

16. Henri Desroche (above, note 8), pp. 19-47, 161-92.

17. For a detailed discussion of the censorship of *Le Nouveau Monde industriel et sociétaire*, see Michel Butor's introduction to the work (Paris, 1973).

18. Barthes (above, note 11), p. 99.

19. Sketches are not uncommon in Fourier. See, e.g., IX, 574-75: dialogue between a grocer trying to sell vermicelli (which Fourier detested) and a tired housewife; Xa, 240-48: a playlet about the Stock Exchange; Xb, 340-47: a dialogue between God and mortals.

20. Bernardin de Saint-Pierre, *Etudes de la nature, Etude XI*: "Harmonies végétales des plantes avec l'homme."

21. E.g., IV, 4 (Everybody is wrong about Man's destiny; how could they not be wrong, when they use musical notation based on eleven lines instead of twelve?); Xa, 335-40 (On the importance of our little planet in our solar system, which is musically organized. What has this to do with the previous section [on European politics]? Everything, since "everything is linked in the system of nature" [p. 340], and one can only understand the social order by reference to, among others, the planetary or aromal one, coordinating them with geometrical theorems.)

22. See Chapter 3.

23. IX, 830-34, based on an article by George Sand in the *Revue des Deux Mondes*, November 15, 1836 ("Lettres d'un voyageur").

24. E.g., I, 157; IV, 372, IV, 557; V, 236; VII, 157. Life in Harmony is a breathless affair; cf. Fourier's remarks on keeping people busy (VII, 170) and keeping time (IV, 372).

25. I, pp. 10, 13, 14, 17, 20, 26; III, pp. 2, 16, 60, 71-72, 107, 369, etc., VIII, *passim*.

26. See Desroche, pp. 19-47; Manuel (above, note 2), pp. 244-45; R. Bonnain-Moerdyck, "Fourier gastrosophe," in *Actualité de Fourier* (1975), pp. 163-68.

27. See Chapter 4.

28. Jonathan Culler, *Structuralist Poetics* (London, 1975), chapter on

"Convention and Naturalization," from which these quotations are taken.

29. Barthes, pp. 95, 7-11.
30. Culler, *Structuralist Poetics*, ibid.
31. See Chapter 2.
32. Barthes, p. 16.

Chapter Two

1. Paris, Institut National d'Histoire Sociale, 14 AS 7. For a detailed study of the genesis of the *Great Treatise* and its relationship to the *Théorie de l' unité universelle*, see Emile Poulat, *Les Cahiers manuscrits de Charles Fourier* (1957), esp. pp. 66-74.

2. The Enlightenment is the name normally given to the flowering (in the eighteenth century) of the belief in natural law, universal order, and the rational nature and goodness of Man.

3. For a consideration of possible influences of these authors, see below, Chapter 9.

4. See Janina Rose Mailer, "Fourier et Marx," in *Actualité de Fourier*, p. 251. For a detailed discussion of Fourier and religion, see Henri Desroche, *Les Dieux rêvés, théisme et athéisme en utopie* (1972), pp. 89-145.

5. See M. C. Spencer, "Charles Fourier: la musique savante scande notre désir," *Australian Journal of French Studies*, XI: 3(1974), 253-62.

6. E.g., I, 67, n. 1: "It is not arbitrarily that the King's foot [approx. $\frac{1}{3}$ meter] indicates it [seven feet: the average height of humans in Harmony] as a natural measure; it has this property because it is equal to 1/32 of the height of water in suction pumps." For counting by twelves, see IV, 586; VI, 482; IX, 529, etc., and below, Chapter 7, note 7.

7. See Chapter 6.

8. Simone Debout, Introduction to Charles Fourier, *Théorie des quatre mouvements*, p. 23.

9. See Chapter 9.

10. See Jonathan Beecher and Richard Bienvenu, *The Utopian Vision of Charles Fourier* (Boston, 1971), p. 216, n.1, for a discussion of the range of connotations suggested by the terms.

11. See Chapter 5 for Fourier's discussion of the case of Mme Strogonoff.

12. The difficulty in organizing society so as to accord with Man's desires is that they must be known in advance. See Chapter 8 for a discussion of the potential dangers of prediction.

13. See Chapter 6 esp. section III.

Chapter Three

1. See Chapter 6.
2. I, 52-56. See also VII, 154-62, IX, 805/19-20/Y9 and 466/x-69/x. The detail varies slightly, but the overall picture is the same.
3. The following sources have been used for the information given above: F. Armand and R. Maublanc, *Fourier* (1937), Vol 1., pp. 9-37; H. Bourgin, *Fourier: contribution à l'étude du socialisme français* (1905), pp. 34-47; G. Dupeux, *La Société française 1789-1970* (1972), pp. 67-79, 132, 135.
4. Fourier, like many writers of the Enlightenment, was struck by the variability of moral codes in different countries. See, e.g., IX, 560, 566.
5. XII, 559-62. The Catholic Church is blamed, among other things, for its "antivoluptuousness," its toleration of slavery, and its obscurantism.
6. See also XII, 660-66: "The Relationship between Morality and Religion."
7. See Chapter 9.
8. See Pascal Bruckner, *Fourier* (1975), pp. 54-56, for a brilliant discussion of this point.
9. *Recueil d'articles*, part 6, pp. 117-19 ("De la Méthode mixte en étude de l'attraction"). The italics used above are Fourier's.
10. Fourier was as violently anti-Semitic as he was anti-English, mainly because of the Jews' success in commerce. See, e.g., I, 60-61; II, 169 (first pagination); IV, 279; V, 24, n.1, etc., and, among the unpublished writings, Xa, 243, 272; Xb, 225; XIa, 32-37, where Fourier states that the principle of religious tolerance should be transgressed in respect of the Jews. For a detailed discussion of Fourier's anti-Semitism, see E. Silberner, "Charles Fourier on the Jewish Question," *Jewish Social Studies*, VIII (1946), 245-66.
11. I, 249. See also VI, 394, XIa, 26-32. Fourier is referring to the proliferation of food substitutes under the Empire, brought about by the prohibition of imports (see Armand and Maublanc [above, note 3], pp. 27-29).
12. See also IV, 121-26; VI, 396-402, for further details of bankruptcy.
13. Long hours contravened the "butterfly" principle, which demanded frequent changes of task. See, e.g., VI, 74, and below, Chapter 4.
14. Jules Michelet's *Le Peuple* (1846) is a classic work on the French people, with long sections on the "bondage" of peasants, factory workers, and others.
15. Beecher and Bienvenu, *The Utopian Vision of Charles Fourier*, p. 30, quoting I, 67. See also V, 553.
16. See Chapter 9.
17. See Chapter 2.

18. E.g., V, 502; V, 563 ("Nature gives nothing to him who has nothing"); VI, 122.

19. In the "Lettre au grand Juge" (Letter to the High Judge), 4 Nivôse, an XI (December 26, 1803: an XI should be an XII), translated by Beecher and Bienvenu, pp. 83-93.

20. See Chapter 8.

Chapter Four

1. On "reduced" or "simple" Phalanxes, see, e.g., VI, 380; VIII, 76; IX, 617/N; XII, 217-365 ("On Serisophy").

2. VI, 110-11, table reproduced in a simplified form, "for compelling typographical reasons," by Beecher and Bienvenu, p. 256.

3. VI, 340-44.

4. Brillat-Savarin, *Physiologie du goût* (1965), p. 23.

5. These calculations vary considerably. For instance, five is later given as the minimum number of groups in a series, with seven as the minimum number of members of a group, and nine as the perfect number (VI, 59).

6. III, 15. The six other conditions and the "pivotal" one are: 1. That each worker should be paid by dividend, as opposed to salary. 2. The remuneration should be proportional to the worker's contribution of capital, work, and talent. 3. Varied, short work sessions. 4. Pleasantness of work surroundings. 5. Suitable tasks for all. 6. The right to participate in whatever work one is qualified to carry out. ✕ A minimum income.

7. Jean Goret, *La Pensée de Fourier* (1974), p. 104.

8. The first objection was formulated in 1879 by Paul Janet, who is quoted by Riasanovsky, p. 198. The second is by Emile Lehouck, *Fourier aujourd'hui* (1966), p. 83.

9. See also V, 400; Xa, 102, 191-93.

10. VI, 68 (italics and capitalization as in text). See also V, 537-41, on Cléon's day.

11. Very inefficient series are known as "eclipsed," and carry a black banner during parades (Xa, 149, n.1).

12. See also Chapter 2.

13. V, 352-59; VII, 339-79.

14. Fourier's "orality" is mentioned by R. Bonnain-Moerdyck, "Fourier gastrosophe," in *Actualité de Fourier*, p. 146, n.5.

15. V, 558; VI, 355; IX, 811.

16. Antipodean readers will doubtless be reacting to this with delight. It should be clear, however, that the Harmonian meat pie, with its endless varieties, is a kind of Platonic reply to the insipid Australian product.

17. For the Little Hordes, see Chapter 5.

18. See Chapter 1, note 24.

19. For discussion of space in Fourier and "normal" Utopian space, see Chapter 8.

20. Michel Butor, "L'Espace du roman," in *Répertoire II* (1964), p. 49.

21. See below, Chapter 7.

22. Fourier's dislike of tne Chinese is similarly motivated to his dislike of the Jews. See, e.g., I, 59-60; VI, 418, Xa, 272.

23. VI, 349. See also IV, 188-90; V, 537.

Chapter Five

1. See C.-G. Dubois, *Problèmes de l'utopie* (1968), p. 45.

2. For Fourier's views on education, see David Zeldin, *The Educational Ideas of Charles Fourier* (London, 1969).

3. In a passage published posthumously (Xb, 298), Fourier emphasizes the development of "compound" (corporeal and spiritual) vigor as the main aim of education.

4. Fourier believed that the tactile sense was underdeveloped until puberty, as it was mainly concerned with erotic activity, which for him did not begin until then (V, 76).

5. For further details on "compound hygiene" or the "medicine of taste," see VI, 260-61; VII, 127-30.

6. For the delayed anality of the Little Hordes, see Jean Goret, *La Pensée de Fourier*, pp. 114-15.

7. The translation cannot do justice to the French here, as Fourier invents a masculine word ("vestel"), using a feminine root ("vestale").

8. The study of analogy is also a powerful distraction or "bait" (V, 135). See Chapter 2.

9. Fourier's experience at Belley, when, as a man in his mid-forties, he apparently had to (or chose to) keep his teenage nieces at bay, may be responsible for this.

10. A useful "balance-sheet" will be found in Zeldin (above, note 2), Chapter 10, most of whose conclusions we agree with.

11. René Schérer, *Charles Fourier ou la contestation globale* (1970), p. 92.

12. See also Chapter 9.

13. Simone Debout, "L'Illusion réelle," *Topique*, 4-5 (October 1970), 11-78 (analysis of episode pp. 42-78); Catherine Francblin, "Le Féminisme utopique de Charles Fourier," *Tel Quel*, 62 (Summer 1975), 44-69.

14. Some of the captives are male, in an ironic reversal of the various forms of captivity affecting females in Civilization, as Fourier points out (VII, 170-71).

15. Francblin, pp. 66-67.

16. Frank Manuel, *The Prophets of Paris*, p. 248.

Chapter Six

1. Paris, Archives Nationales, 10 AS 6. Reproduced in J. Beecher, "L'Archibras de Fourier: Un manuscrit censuré," *La Brèche*, (1964), 66-71.

2. Catherine Francblin (Chapter 5, note 13), p. 59.

3. Emile Lehouck, *Fourier aujourd'hui* (1966), pp. 131-57. See also Hélène Tuzet, "Deux types de cosmogonies vitalistes: 2.—Charles Fourier, Hygiéniste du cosmos," *Revue des Sciences Humaines*, 101 (Jan-Mar 1961), 37-47.

4. A. Cioranescu, *L'Avenir du passé* (1972), pp. 198-203.

5. See Chapter 2.

6. Victor Hugo, *Les Contemplations*: "Saturne"; "Explication"; "Ce que dit la bouche d'ombre," etc.

7. Simone Debout, Introduction to *Fourier, Œuvres Complètes* (1966), Vol. 1., p. xxii.

8. It is clear from this that Fourier, like Balzac, was familiar with the theories of animal magnetism developed by Franz Mesmer at the end of the eighteenth century.

9. See Chapter 9.

10. "Cosmogony" is the theory of the generation of the universe; "cosmology" is the theory of the laws governing the universe.

11. All of these, with the exception of Venus, are in fact asteroids.

12. Lehouck (above, note 3), p. 148.

13. Raymond Queneau, "Les Ennemis de la lune," in *Bords* (1963), p. 56, n.1.

14. Pascal, *Pensées* in *Œuvres complètes* (1954), p. 1113 ("Pensée" no. 91).

15. Tuzet (above, note 3), pp. 44-45.

16. E.g., the 600,000 athletes armed with 300,000 bottles celebrating Apicius's triumph (V, 358), or the saving of 400,000,000,000 francs per annum on a global basis if one is careful with pins and matches (IV, 208).

Chapter Seven

1. See Chapter 1.

2. Most of these relationships are explained in IV, 356-59. See also Henri Desroche, *La Société festive*, pp. 96-98.

3. Michel Butor, "Le Féminin chez Fourier," in *Répertoire IV* (1974), 193-207, esp. 202-203.

4. See Chapter 2.

5. Simone Debout, appendix to *Charles Fourier, Théorie des quatre mouvements* (1967), p. 389. We are not convinced that the equivalences she gives are correct.

6. This is (unfortunately) *not* the modern twelve-tone system. See M. C. Spencer (Chapter 2, note 5), p. 261.

7. Fourier chose twelve because it and its multiples have the greatest number of divisers. Some of his calculations become clearer when we realize that, for example, 144 = either 12 x 12 or 10 x 10, there being two new, unspecified symbols between 9 and 10. See René Schérer, *Charles Fourier ou la contestation globale*, p. 72.

8. Simone Debout, *"Griffe au nez" ou donner "have ou art"* (1974). The manuscript was first published by J. Beecher in *La Brèche*, 4, (1963), 24-25, and is reproduced in Lehouck, *Fourier aujourd'hui*, p. 255.

9. Quoted by Samuel Levin, *Linguistic Structures in Poetry* (The Hague, 1962), p. 49.

10. Jean Starobinski, *Les Mots sous les mots* (1971), pp. 117, 121-54.

11. See Chapter 2.

12. Notably by Hubert Juin, "Présence de Fourier dans la poésie moderne," *Topique*, 4-5 (October 1970), 103-25.

13. For the semantics of metaphor see J.-M. Adam and J.-P. Goldenstein, *Linguistique et discours littéraire* (1976), pp. 42-48; Umberto Eco, "Sémantique de la métaphore," *Tel Quel*, 55 (Autumn 1973), 25-46.

14. By "compared" and "comparer" are meant, respectively, the initial term, and the term which is brought in for comparative purposes. See also the remarks of Jean Ricardou (below, note 17).

15. We are grateful to a colleague, Professor Les Holborow, of the University of Queensland Philosophy Department, for helping us to unscramble Fourier's logic.

16. Umberto Eco (above, note 13), p. 30.

17. Jean Ricardou, *Problèmes du nouveau roman* (1967), p. 134.

18. Michel Foucault, *Les Mots et les choses* (1966), pp. 40-45.

19. Roland Barthes, *Sade, Fourier, Loyola*, pp. 96-100.

20. André Breton, quoted by Hubert Juin (above, note 12), p. 109.

Chapter Eight

1. For Saint-Simon and Owen, see Chapter 1 (*Pièges et charlatanisme . . .*) For Fénelon, see V, 477-85.

2. C.-G. Dubois, *Problèmes de l'utopie*, p. 17. See also Georges Duveau, *Sociologie de l'utopie*, (1961), pp. 97-107.

3. Gilles Lapouge, *Utopie et civilisations* (1973), pp. 103-104.

4. Lapouge, pp. 15-16.

5. Roger Mucchielli, *Le Mythe de la cité idéale* (1960), p. 177.

6. Mucchielli, p. 177.

7. Lapouge, pp. 138-39, classifies Rabelais as a counter-utopian.

8. Dubois (above, note 2), p. 35.

9. Mucchielli (above, note 5), pp. 55-74, distinguishes six dialectical phases in the formation of Utopia, contrasting More's Utopianism with the "political realism" of Machiavelli.

10. Dubois, p. 54.

11. Alexandre Cioranescu, *L'Avenir du passé: utopie et littérature* (1972), p. 23; Louis Marin, *Utopiques, jeux d'espace* (1973), pp. 53-86.

12. Marin, p. 157.

13. For reviews of theories of "narrative grammar" or "narrative morphology" see Jonathan Culler, *Structuralist Poetics*, pp. 205-224; J.-M. Adam and J.-P. Goldenstein, *Linguistique et discours littéraire*, pp. 213-25.

14. Dominique Desanti, *Les Socialistes de l'utopie* (1970), p. 314.

15. On the desire for verisimilitude see Raymond Trousson, "Utopie et roman utopique," *Revue des Sciences Humaines*, 155 (1974), 367-78; on distanciation, see C.-G. Dubois, "Une architecture fixionnelle," ibid., pp. 449-71, and *Problèmes de l'utopie*, p. 39.

16. Dubois, "Une architecture fixionnelle," pp. 461-62.

17. Pascal Bruckner, *Fourier*, p. 184.

18. See Chapter 9.

19. See Chapter 3, note 18.

20. See Chapter 6.

21. Luce Giard, "Voyageuse Raison," *Esprit*, 4 (April 1974), 560.

22. Raymond Trousson, *Voyages aux pays de nulle part* (Brussels, 1975), p. 28.

23. Lapouge, p. 38.

24. E.g., VI, 320 ("mathematical" and "potential"); VI, 132-35 ("grafted"); XIa, 29-36 ("contiguous"); XII, 367-413 ("measured").

25. For the "open-ness" of Fourier's series, see Bruckner, pp. 43, 165; and Simone Debout, *Préface* to *Œuvres Complètes*, VII, pp. xxvii-xxviii, xlvii, cvii.

26. Marin (above, note 11), p. 177.

27. For a brilliant discussion of different kinds of verisimilitude, see Culler (above, note 13), pp. 140-60.

28. Cioranescu (above, note 11), p. 223.

29. "The irregular oscillatory movement of microscopic particles suspended in a limpid fluid" (O.E.D.).

30. One of the alternatives to "Phalanx" used by Fourier is "tourbillon" (whirl), a word which has the same meanings in English as in French: a movement toward the center (as in "whirlpool"), or a bustle of activity. Its different connotations seem appropriate to the contradictory pulls within Fourier's system.

31. Lapouge, p. 231.

Chapter Nine

1. Julia Kristeva, *Semeiotiké: recherches pour une sémanalyse* (1969), p. 146: "every text is constructed as a mosaic of quotations, every text is absorption and transformation of another text."

2. Hippolyte Bourgin, *Fourier. Contribution à l'étude du socialisme français* (1905), Chapter Two.

3. Emile Lehouck, *Fourier aujourd'hui* (1966), pp. 165-72. On Fourier's sources see also Gérald Schaeffer, "L'Ode à Charles Fourier et la tradition," in *André Breton, Essais et témoignages* (Neuchâtel, 1950), pp. 83-109.

4. Bourgin, p. 101. See Fernand Rude, "Genèse et fin d'un mythe historique: le pré-fouriérisme de l'Ange," *Topique*, 4-5 (October 1970), 175-189.

5. For Condillac, see Xa, 30; Newton, VIII, 61; Owen and Saint-Simon, Chapter 1; Rousseau, V, 47; Voltaire, VI, 355. Fourier is of course inconsistent, and Rousseau and Voltaire are sometimes praised explicitly or implicitly: e.g., VIII, 33 (Rousseau) or III, 109 (Voltaire's "But what a dark night envelops nature," which Fourier was always quoting).

6. Nicholas Riasanovsky, *The Teaching of Charles Fourier*, pp. 30-31.

7. Jonathan Beecher and Richard Bienvenu, *The Utopian Vision of Charles Fourier*, p. 234.

8. The "Physiocrats" (François Quesnay, 1694-1774, Vincent de Gournay, 1712-1759, and others) believed that the key to wealth and prosperity lay solely in the proper management of the land.

9. Love is "the passion of unreason" (VIII, 384).

10. See Donald Charlton, *Secular Religions in France 1815-1870* (London, 1963); Paul Bénichou, *Le Temps des prophètes* (1977); Dominique Desanti, *Les Socialistes de l'utopie* (1970).

11. "Epoch [of] passionate search for a system allowing the reconciliation of opposed doctrines . . . in a total science. The dominant Romantic ideas are essentially those of *Unity, Analogy, Development, Harmony*" (Léon Cellier, *Fabre d'Olivet*, quoted by Lehouck, p. 154).

12. Charlton (above, note 10), pp. 126-35.

13. Bourgin, p. 81.

14. Bertrand Russell, *History of Western Philosophy* (London, 1955), pp. 141-53.

15. Hubert Juin, "Présence de Charles Fourier dans la poésie moderne," *Topique* (above, note 4), pp. 103-25, quotation p. 107. See also Lehouck, pp. 153-54, 209-14, and Schaeffer (above, note 3), p. 85.

16. Hélène Tuzet, "Deux types de cosmogonies vitalistes, 1. Restif de

la Bretonne ou le cœur humain dévoilé,'' *Revue des Sciences Humaines,* 100 (1960), 495-506.

17. All of these details are taken from *Les Posthumes* (Paris: chez Duchêne, 1802, 4 volumes). For Fourier on the sun and fire as manifestations of God, see Xb, 211.

18. The examples are taken from the *Œuvres complètes* (1818), vols. VIII-X.

19. Gustave Flaubert, *Bouvard et Pécuchet* (livre de poche, 1959), pp. 225-26.

20. On Fourier and Zola's *Travail*, see Henri Desroche, *La Société festive,* pp. 321-46.

21. Charles Baudelaire, *Œuvres complètes* (1961), pp. 376, 704; *Correspondance* (1973), Vol l., pp. 335-37 (letter dated January 21, 1856).

22. Among Hambly's articles are ''Théophile Gautier et le Fouriérisme,'' *Australian Journal of French Studies,* 3 (1974), 210-36, and ''The Structure of *Les Fleurs du Mal:* another suggestion,'' ibid., 3 (1971), 269-96.

23. André Breton, *Ode à Charles Fourier* (1961), edited by Jean Gaulmier.

24. Hubert Juin (above, note 15), p. 103.

25. Breton, quoted by Juin, p. 109.

26. For Roussel, see, in English, Rayner Heppenstall, *Raymond Roussel* (London, 1966); in French, Bernard Caburet, *Raymond Roussel* (1968), esp. pp. 7-19, 51-60; Michel Foucault, *Raymond Roussel* (1963).

27. Henri Desroche, *La Société festive,* table pp. 202-205.

28. Ibid., p. 199. See also Riasanovsky (above, note 6), pp. 202-205.

29. Riasanovsky, pp. 205-206.

30. Engels to Marx, March 17, 1845, quoted by Roger Dangeville, ed., *Marx-Engels, Utopisme et communauté de l'avenir* (1976), p. 138.

31. Engels, quoted by Roger Dangeville, ed., *Marx-Engels, Les Utopistes* (1976), pp. 54-56.

32. Ibid., pp. 42-43.

33. Ibid., p. 126.

34. Marx quoted by Dangeville (above, note 30), p. 10, n.1.

35. For the concept of work in Fourier and Marx, see Janina Rosa Mailer, ''Fourier et Marx,'' in *Actualité de Fourier,* pp. 264-87.

36. For Fourier and Rousseau, see Lehouck, pp. 80, 92-93; René Schérer, *Charles Fourier ou la contestation globale,* pp. 96-99, and David Zeldin, *The Educational Ideas of Charles Fourier,* pp. 34-35 and *passim.*

37. For most of what follows I have relied on Zeldin, and on Goret, *La Pensée de Fourier,* pp. 111-38.

38. Zeldin, p. 148.

39. See Zeldin, pp. 146-47, on the experiments of A. S. Makarenko; and Jean Goret, ''L'Essai d'une 'Phalangette' d'enfants,'' *Topique,* 4-5

(1970), 191-204 (on an experimental children's home in Moscow).
40. Engels (above, note 30), pp. 126-31, esp. p. 129.
41. Pascal Bruckner and Alain Finkielkraut, *Le Nouveau Désordre amoureux* (Denoël, 1977).
42. Lehouck, p. 34.
43. J. A. C. Brown, *Freud and the Post-Freudians* (Harmondsworth, 1961), p. 30.
44. Jean Goret, *La Pensée de Fourier*, p. 114.
45. Jonathan Beecher and Richard Bienvenu, *The Utopian Vision of Charles Fourier*, p. 330.

Chapter Ten

1. Mailer (Chapter 9, note 35), pp. 260-61, claims that the Harmonians are intellectually and emotionally immature.
2. Johan Huizinga, *Homo Ludens* (London, 1970), p. 27; Sigmund Freud, *Beyond the Pleasure Principle*, in *The Complete Works*, Vol. XVIII (London, 1955); Norman Brown, *Life against Death* (London, 1959).
3. Brown, pp. 307, 318. See also Pierre Klossowski, "Sade et Fourier," *Topique*, 4-5 (1970), 90.
4. George Steiner, Introduction to Huizinga, *Homo Ludens*, p. 15.

Selected Bibliography

The place of publication is Paris unless otherwise stated.

PRIMARY SOURCES

Œuvres complètes. 12 Volumes, Editions Anthropos, 1966-68, as follows:

Vol. 1. *Théorie des quatre mouvements et des destinées générales,* with an introduction by Simone Debout-Oleszkiewicz (anastatic reprint of the third edition, 1846).

Vols. 2-5. *Théorie de l'unité universelle* (anastatic reprint of the second edition, 1842).

Vol. 6. *Le Nouveau Monde industriel et sociétaire,* with a preface by Simone Debout-Oleszkiewicz (anastatic reprint of the second edition, 1845).

Vol. 7. *Le Nouveau Monde amoureux,* based on unpublished manuscripts. Arrangement, notes, and introduction by Simone Debout-Oleszkiewicz, with an original drawing by Matta.

Vols. 8-9. *La Fausse Industrie morcelée, répugnante, mensongère, et l'antidote, l'industrie naturelle, combinée, attrayante, véridique, donnant quadruple produit et perfection extrême en toutes qualités. Mosaïque des faux progrès, des ridicules et cercles vicieux de la Civilisation. Parallèle des deux mondes industriels, l'ordre morcelé et l'ordre combiné* (anastatic reprint of the two-volume edition, 1835-1836).

Vols. 10-11. *Manuscrits publiés par la Phalange* (volume 10 contains a), manuscripts published by *La Phalange,* 1851, and b), 1852. Volume 11 contains a) manuscripts published by *La Phalange* 1853-1856, and b), 1856-1858).

Vol. 12. *Manuscrits publiés par la Phalange* (various manuscripts, published between 1845 and 1849).

Le Nouveau Monde industriel et sociétaire. Preface by Michel Butor. Flammarion, Nouvelle Bibliothèque Romantique, 1973.

Recueil d'articles extraits de la 'Phalange, Revue de la Science Sociale.' Librairie phalanstérienne, 1849. Contains approximately half the manuscripts published in Vol. 12 of the *Œuvres complètes,* plus other important pieces from *La Phalange.*

Théorie des quatre mouvements et des destinées générales. Introduction, notes, and glossary of terms by Simone Debout. Also contains extracts from *Le Nouveau Monde amoureux.* Pauvert, 1967.

Archives Nationales, no. 10 AS : twenty-five boxes and bundles containing Fourier's correspondence, manuscripts, etc. See Emile Poulat, *Les Cahiers manuscrits de Charles Fourier*, BELC/Minuit, 1957.

Institut Français d'Histoire Sociale, no. 14 AS: *Fonds fouriériste*: various periodicals, pamphlets, books, etc., stored under appalling conditions in an attic.

The Utopian Vision of Charles Fourier, Selected Texts on Work, Love, and Passionate Attraction. Translated, edited, and with an introduction by Jonathan Beecher and Richard Bienvenu. Boston, Mass.: Beacon Press, 1971. Essential for the reader with no French, and excellent in all respects.

SECONDARY SOURCES

1. Books on Fourier

Actualité de Fourier, Colloque d'Arc-et-Senans. Anthropos, 1975. Papers on Fourier from the 1972 colloquium.

BARTHES, ROLAND. *Sade, Fourier, Loyola.* Seuil, 1971. Section on Fourier is quite brilliant.

BOURGIN, HUBERT. *Fourier, Contribution à l'étude du socialisme français.* Société Nouvelle de Librairie et d'Edition, 1905. Doctoral thesis, with very full bibliography of Fourier's writings. Plays down Fourier's sources.

BRETON, ANDRÉ. *Ode à Charles Fourier.* Ed. by Jean Gaulmier. Klincksieck, 1961.

BRUCKNER, PASCAL. *Fourier.* Seuil, Coll. Ecrivains de Toujours, 1975. Concentrates on Fourier's writings on love. Well illustrated.

BUTOR, MICHEL. *La Rose des vents. 32 Rhumbs pour Charles Fourier.* Gallimard, Coll. le Chemin, 1970. Poetic extension of Fourier's cosmogony.

DEBOUT, SIMONE. *'Griffe au nez' ou donner 'have ou art,' écriture inconnue de Charles Fourier.* Anthropos, 1974. Reproduces, with detailed commentary, Fourier's homophonous manuscript.

DESROCHE, HENRI. *La Société festive: du fouriérisme écrit aux fouriérismes pratiqués.* Seuil, 1975. Comprehensive account of the fortunes of Fourierism in France and elsewhere, particularly the United States.

GORET, JEAN. *La Pensée de Fourier.* P.U.F., Coll. SUP, 1974. Excellent introduction, especially to Fourier as a social thinker.

LEHOUCK, EMILE. *Fourier aujourd'hui.* Denoël, Coll. Dossiers des Lettres Nouvelles, 1966. Still the best introduction to Fourier in French.

MANUEL, FRANK. *The Prophets of Paris.* Cambridge, Mass.: Harvard University Press, 1962. Contains brilliant chapter on Fourier's personality and works.

PELLARIN, CHARLES. *Charles Fourier, sa vie et sa théorie.* 2nd ed. Librairie de l'Ecole sociétaire, 1843. This is the fullest of the five editions, but see our remarks in Chapter 1, note 1.

RIASANOVSKY, NICHOLAS V. *The Teaching of Charles Fourier.* Berkeley and Los Angeles: University of California Press, 1969. Very reliable, comprehensive introduction to Fourier's thought.

SCHÉRER, RENÉ. *Charles Fourier ou la contestation globale.* Seghers, Coll. Philosophes de tous les temps, 1970. Contains extracts from Fourier's writings.

SILBERLING, EMILE. *Dictionnaire de sociologie phalanstérienne.* Rivière, 1911. Alphabetical dictionary of Fourier's terminology, with refs. to works. Several important terms not included, however.

VERGEZ, ANDRÉ. *Fourier.* PUF, Coll. SUP Philosophes, 1969.

ZELDIN, DAVID. *The Educational Ideas of Charles Fourier.* London: Cass and Co., 1969. Drab but reliable presentation of Fourier's educational ideas.

2. Articles on Fourier

BEECHER, JONATHAN. "L'Archibras de Fourier: un manuscrit censuré," *La Brèche,* 7 (1964), 66-71.

BUTOR, MICHEL. "Le Feminin chez Fourier," *Répertoire IV,* Gallimard, 1974, pp. 193-207.

DEBOUT, SIMONE. "L'Illusion réelle," *Topique,* 4-5 (October 1970), 11-78.

DESANTI, DOMINIQUE. "San Francisco: Des Hippies pour Fourier," *Topique,* 4-5 (October 1970), 205-12.

FRANCBLIN, CATHERINE. "Le Féminisme utopique de Charles Fourier," *Tel Quel,* 62 (Summer 1975), 44-69.

GORET, JEAN. "L'Essai d'une 'Phalangette' d'enfants," *Topique,* 4-5 (October 1970), 191-204.

HAMBLY, PETER. "Théophile Gautier et le fouriérisme," *Australian Journal of French Studies,* XI:3 (1974), 210-36.

_____. "The Structure of *Les Fleurs du Mal*: Another Suggestion," *Australian Journal of French Studies,* VIII:3 (1971), 269-96.

JUIN, HUBERT. "Présence de Charles Fourier dans la poésie moderne," *Topique,* 4-5 (October 1970), 63-125.

KLOSSOWSKI, PIERRE. "Sade et Fourier," *Topique,* 4-5 (October 1970), 79-98.

MALENGREZ, MICHEL. "Fourier et la métaphore," *Communications,* 19 (1972), 148-54.

QUENEAU, RAYMOND. "Dialectique hégélienne et séries de Fourier," in

Bords, Hermann, 1963, pp. 37-51.

————. "Les Ennemis de la lune," in *Bords*, pp. 53-57.

RUDE, FERNAND. "Genèse et fin d'un mythe historique: le pré-fouriérisme de l'Ange," *Topique*, 4-5 (October 1970), 175-89.

SCHAEFFER, GÉRALD. "L'Ode à Charles Fourier et la Tradition." In Marc Eigeldinger ed. *André Breton, Essais et témoignages*. Neuchâtel: A la Baconnière, 1950, pp. 83-109.

SILBERNER, EMILE. "Charles Fourier on the Jewish Question," *Jewish Social Studies*, VIII:4 (1946), 245-66.

SPENCER, MICHAEL. "Butor et Fourier," in *Butor: Colloque de Cerisy*. Union Générale des Editions, 1974, pp. 203-14.

————. "Charles Fourier: la musique savante scande notre désir," *Australian Journal of French Studies*, XI:3 (1974), 253-62.

TUZET, HÉLÈNE. "Deux Types de cosmogonies vitalistes. 2.—Charles Fourier, hygiéniste du cosmos," *Revue des Sciences Humaines*, 101 (Jan.-Mar. 1961), 37-47.

ZILBERFARB, I. "L'Imagination et la réalité dans l'oeuvre de Fourier," *Le Mouvement social*, 60 (1967), 5-21.

3. Books and Articles on Utopia

Australian Journal of French Studies, Vol. XI:3 (1974). Special number on Utopia and Socialism, containing articles on Fourier by Simone Debout, Peter Hambly, and Michael Spencer.

CIORANESCU, ALEXANDRE. *L'Avenir du passé, utopie et littérature*. Gallimard, Coll. Les Essais. 1972.

DESROCHE, HENRI. *Les Dieux rêvés, théisme et athéisme en utopie*. Desclée de Brauwer, 1972. Contains a long chapter on Fourier and religion.

Le Discours utopique. Union Générale des Editions, 1978. *Acta* of a colloquium at the Centre Culturel International, Cerisy-la-Salle, France, 1975. Papers by C.-G. Dubois, Pierre Ansart, Simone Debout, M. Le Doeuff, and René Schérer are of particular interest for Fourier.

DUBOIS, CLAUDE-GILBERTE. *Problèmes de l'utopie*. Minard, Coll. Archives des Lettres Modernes, no. 85, 1968. Short, clear introduction to many aspects of Utopia.

DUVEAU, GEORGES. *Sociologie de l'utopie*. P.U.F., 1961.

Esprit, 4 (April 1974). Special number on Utopia.

LAPOUGE, GILLES. *Utopie et Civilisations*. Weber, 1973. Illuminating, sometimes unusual views. Complements very well works by Dubois and Trousson.

Littérature, 21 (February 1976). Special number on "lieux de l'utopie."

MARIN, LOUIS. *Utopiques, jeux d'espace*. Minuit, 1973. Semiotic analysis of Utopias based on Thomas More, *Utopia.*

MARX, KARL, and ENGELS, FRIEDRICH. *Les Utopistes.* Introduction, translation, and notes by Roger Dangeville. Maspero. 1976. Critical anthology of writings on Utopia by Marx and Engels.

————. *Utopisme et communauté de l'avenir.* Introduction, translation, and notes by Roger Dangeville. Maspero, 1976. As preceding work.

MUCCHIELLI, ROGER. *Le Mythe de la cité idéale.* P.U.F., 1960. Fairly severe on Fourier as a social thinker.

Revue des Sciences Humaines, 155 (1974). Special number on Utopia.

TROUSSON, RAYMOND. *Voyages aux pays de nulle part: Histoire littéraire de la pensée utopique.* Brussels: Université Libre de Bruxelles, Publications de la Faculté de Philosophie et Lettres, no. 60, 1975. Solid but not very exciting historical review of (usually not very exciting) Utopias.

4. Background Works

BÉNICHOU, PAUL. *Le Temps des prophètes.* Gallimard, Coll. Bibliothèque des Idées, 1977. On neo-Catholicism, pseudoscientific Utopianism, and other currents of social and religious thought in France from 1800-1850. Includes a short section on Fourier.

CHARLTON, DONALD. *Secular Religions in France, 1815-1870.* London: Oxford University Press for University of Hull, 1963. Stresses the religious aspect of social Romanticism. Section on Fourier.

DESANTI, DOMINIQUE. *Les Socialistes de l'utopie.* Payot, Coll. Petite Bibliothèque Payot, 1970. Very useful work containing texts by Fourier, Saint-Simon, Owen, Cabet, and others.

DUPEUX, GEORGES. *La Société française 1789-1870.* Armand Colin, Coll. U, 1972.

VIATTE, AUGUSTE. *Les Sources occultes du romantisme.* Champion, 1969 (new edition). Interesting on Fourier and Restif de la Bretonne.

5. Addendum

LEHOUCK, EMILE. *Vie de Charles Fourier.* Denoël/Gonthier, Coll. Médiations, 1978. Long awaited, but rather disappointing on a first reading. Highly critical of Pellarin and other early biographers, but still relies quite heavily on them. Reasonably convincing picture of a less solitary and less repressed Fourier than, e.g., Manuel presents. The problem is still that we do not know very much about Fourier's life.

Glossary

Accord. Harmony within a group or series, which are formed of "Accords and *discords*" (q.v.).

Ambiguous. Transitional, exceptional, enabling *series* (q.v.) to be united or "enmeshed." Ambiguous tastes (*manias*, q.v.) or species have a vital role to play in the functioning of the various *movements* (q.v.), particularly the social one.

Attraction (passionate). The basis of Fourier's system. The force of desire, fundamentally opposed to reason. The *series* (q.v.) are a means of utilizing it for the good of humanity.

Butterfly. A "distributive" passion; the need for change and variety.

Cabalist(ic). Another distributive passion; the need to engage in intrigue.

Civilization. The fifth of the thirty-two social periods, characterized by self-contradiction and stagnation, because the germs of progress toward *Harmony* (q.v.) are unrecognized.

Combined. Pertaining to *Harmony* (q.v.), e.g. "combined order."

Composite. The third distributive passion. A kind of blind enthusiasm involving the senses and the soul, and linked especially with love.

Compound. Combining the spiritual and the material.

Course of pleasure ("parcours"). A combination of pleasures enjoyed successively in a short space of time and enhancing one another. Duration and variety are therefore of more importance than a peak of intensity.

Discord. is opposed by Fourier to "discorde," which is a negative, destructive force. Discord and accord are necessary for the series properly to function. Jean Goret (*La Pensée de Fourier*, p. 137) glosses it as "harmonious difference."

Familyism. One of the minor, "affective" passions tolerated rather than approved by Fourier, who was strongly critical of the family as a social unit.

Gastrosophy. Not classified as a passion by Fourier, but vitally important to the social order. The art of refined overeating, and "the mainspring of Attraction" (VI, 382).

Harmony. Fourier's Utopian social order, characterized by the universal satisfaction of all desires, harmonized by the *series* (q.v.) for the benefit of society.

Mania. Strange, minority desire (e.g. eating live spiders), frequently but not invariably of a sexual nature. The latter type would probably be called perversions today. Vitally important, as it can help to enmesh series.

Movements. Four, sometimes five, domains of creation: the social, the animal, the organic, the material, the aromal. Fourier is mainly concerned with the first, which is the principal or *"pivotal"* (q.v.) one.

Phalanstery. The chief building of a Phalanx, probably inspired architecturally by the Palais-Royal in Paris.

Phalanx. The basically agricultural economic and social unit in Harmony, usually containing around 1600 men, women, and children.

Philosophy, philosophers. A generalized term of abuse, referring to (the doctrines of) philosophers, economists, politicians, and, in general, contemporary thinkers.

Pivot. The central, most important element in, e.g., the series, the social mechanism, etc.

Series. A grouping, carefully calculated according to the exigencies of accord and discord, whereby a number of objects or people are brought together or harmonized, as in a choir.

Seristery. The parts of the Phalanstery used for bringing the various passionate series together.

Unityism. The pivotal passion resulting from the combination of the twelve radical passions.

Whirl ("tourbillon"). A synonym of Phalanx.

Work-Exchange. The daily meeting at which, thanks to the activities of "brokers," thousands of intrigues are combined and the following day's work and amorous timetable are arranged.

⤬Κ꙰Υ⅄ Symbols indicating, respectively, the pivot; ambiguous or transitional ascending (group); ambiguous or transitional descending; ascending subpivot; descending subpivot (see VI, 64-65).

Index